"Thank you, Elyse. The gospel for yesterday but also for today and tomorrow. What you wrote is inspirational, and it overflows with practical application that pushes me to take the gospel into the otherwise private corners of my life. You said in the book, 'This message will be the only message I'll ever have from now on.' If that is the case, I am already in line for the next one."
> —Edward T. Welch, counselor and faculty member,
> Christian Counseling & Education Foundation

"*Because He Loves Me* will provide hope and a desperately needed supply of 'spiritual oxygen' to many Christians who have lost sight of what they have and who they are in Christ and are struggling to live a life they can never live apart from him. We can never afford to move 'past' the gospel message of the love of God through Christ."
> —Nancy Leigh DeMoss; author; radio host, *Revive Our Hearts*

"Elyse Fitzpatrick has given us a helpful, encouraging, and stimulating book that explores the practical impact of God's great love for his people in every aspect of Christian living. Her rich insights into God's revealed truth, when understood and applied, will certainly equip and inspire Christians to better fulfill their chief end of glorifying and enjoying him forever!"
> —Carol J. Ruvolo, author of *Grace to Stand Firm; Grace to Grow;*
> and *No Other Gospel: Finding True Freedom in the Message
> of Galatians*

"The Spirit of God seems to be initiating a widespread recovery of the gospel and its implications. The centrality of the gospel in the ministry of the local church and the life of a Christian is being rediscovered, proclaimed, and enjoyed in place after place, person after person. *Because He Loves Me* is another—and welcome—indication that fresh gospel breezes are blowing. If you love the gospel of Jesus Christ, you'll love what Elyse Fitzpatrick has written in this book.
> —Donald S. Whitney, Professor of Biblical Spirituality,
> The Southern Baptist Theological Seminary; author,
> *Spiritual Disciplines for the Christian Life*

"Many Christian books focus our gaze on the difficult duties of the Christian life, leaving us either triumphant in self-righteous pride or burdened down with a backpack full of guilt. Elyse Fitzpatrick shows us how to lay down that burden of guilt at the cross and put to death that self-righteousness, not merely once but daily, as we glory increasingly in the gospel. Here is profound and practical wisdom that will leave you equipped to face life and death with joyful confidence in God's love for you in Jesus Christ."
> —Iain Duguid, Professor of Old Testament, Grove City College

"Elyse Fitzpatrick reminds us why the gospel is such good news—not only when we hear it for the first time, but even after a lifetime of familiarity with the message. This is a moving exposition of gospel truth showing how the doctrinal content of our faith is not merely dry, academic stuff but wonderfully personal and practical truth. And the gospel message is not just the foundation of our new life in Christ but the bricks and mortar as well. It is therefore relevant not only at the start of our walk with Christ but every day thereafter. That simple but crucial truth is all too often missed in the church today."

—Philip R. Johnson, Executive Director, Grace to You

"We believe our friend Elyse Fitzpatrick has written her magnum opus. This excellent book can be likened to John Piper's *Desiring God* and C. J. Mahaney's *Living the Cross-Centered Life* in the way it shines a refreshing light on the gospel and reminds us of its impact on our life and ministry. This book is amazingly practical while deeply theological. It is destined to become a classic!"

—Pastor Lance and Beth Quinn, The Bible Church of Little Rock, Little Rock, Arkansas

"God has once again gifted Elyse to explain and apply the gospel of Jesus Christ to one's Christian walk and struggles. She helps the reader see that the gospel is not just for salvation but also vital for the believer's everyday life. While many books emphasize the gospel message while neglecting its practical implications, Elyse weds the two together like the New Testament epistles do, continually pointing readers to Jesus Christ and their identity in him. Don't miss out on this uplifting book!"

—Stuart W. Scott, Associate Professor of Biblical Counseling, Southern Baptist Theological Seminary

BECAUSE HE LOVES ME

BECAUSE HE LOVES ME

How Christ Transforms Our Daily Life

ELYSE M. FITZPATRICK

CROSSWAY WHEATON, ILLINOIS

Because He Loves Me: How Christ Transforms Our Daily Life

Copyright ©2008 by Elyse M. Fitzpatrick

Published by Crossway Books
        a publishing ministry of Good News Publishers
        1300 Crescent Street
        Wheaton, Illinois 60187

Cover photo: Veer & iStock

First printing 2008

Printed in the United States of America

Unless otherwise indicated, Scripture quotations are from the ESV® Bible (*The Holy Bible, English Standard Version®*), copyright © 2001 by Crossway Bibles, a publishing ministry of Good News Publishers. Used by permission. All rights reserved.

Scripture references marked NKJV are from *The New King James Version.* Copyright © 1982, Thomas Nelson, Inc. Used by permission.

Scripture references marked NLT are from *The Holy Bible, New Living Translation,* copyright © 1996. Used by permission of Tyndale House Publishers, Inc., Wheaton, Ill., 60189. All rights reserved.

Scripture quotations marked MESSAGE are from *The Message.* Copyright © by Eugene H. Peterson 1993, 1994, 1995, 1996, 2000, 2001, 2002. Used by permission of NavPress Publishing Group.

All emphases in Scripture quotations have been added by the author.

Library of Congress Cataloging-in-Publication Data
Fitzpatrick, Elyse, 1950–
  Because he loves me : how Christ transforms our daily life /
Elyse M. Fitzpatrick.
    p. cm.
  Includes bibliographical references and index.
  ISBN 13: 978-1-58134-905-4 (hc)
  1. Christian women—Religious life. 2. Spirituality. I. Title.
BV4527.F58   2008
248.8'43—dc22   2007044752

LB		19	18	17	16	15	14	13	12	11	10	09
15	14	13	12	11	10	9	8	7	6	5	4	3	2

To

GABRIEL JAMES AND COLIN CHARLES

May you know and love the gospel of Jesus Christ.

CONTENTS

TABLE OF FIGURES

FOREWORD

I have been a born-again Christian for many years now, and God in his kindness has placed me and my family in a Bible believing church where the gospel occupies front and center stage. In the worship music, in the preaching, in home fellowship, in counseling, and in God's people, the Lord Jesus and his work on the cross hold the key position and authority. Yet even with this blessed background and training, I have hit many stumbling blocks of faith. I have had doubts about God's goodness, doubts about God's love, and doubts about overcoming the stubborn, numerous sins that mar my heart, my character, my relationships, and my witness. Yet, through it all, God by a miracle of his grace continues to reveal himself and draw me deeper and closer to him.

One means the Lord used specifically to reveal himself to me was the material Elyse presents here in *Because He Loves Me*. I first heard it in a one-day ladies seminar that preceded a biblical counseling conference. During the conference she presented it again in an abbreviated format tailored for counselors. She demonstrated how the gospel message, in five parts—the incarnation, Jesus' sinless life, his crucifixion, resurrection, and ascension—could be applied practically to a variety of counseling settings such as an anorexic teen and a Christian husband addicted to pornography. It was at this point that the Lord flipped the floodlight of revelation on my heart, and I saw with undisputed clarity that the gospel message is in fact the answer to every problem situation and sin. I, of course, knew this in my head for many years, but God made it an absolute reality in my heart at that minute.

In my mind's eye came the last scene of the movie *The Miracle Worker*, the old version with Patty Duke as little Helen Keller and

Anne Bancroft as Annie Sullivan, the teacher. Throughout the movie, Annie Sullivan has been doggedly persistent in her attempt to teach the blind and deaf Helen sign language. Helen has been alternately angered, depressed, and finally resigned until one moment at the end of the movie, when Ms. Sullivan is signing out the word w-a-t-e-r yet again, the light of understanding goes on in little Helen. There is great drama and emotion as Helen rushes from object to object finally understanding what her patient, loving teacher has been trying to make her understand.

In a similar way to Helen Keller in that last scene, the Lord illuminated my heart to the power of the gospel through Elyse's message that day. Like little Helen, finally understanding, the answer to every question, problem, and sin—the g-o-s-p-e-l, the g-o-s-p-e-l, the g-o-s-p-e-l. Now when I hear it in the worship, my mind signs the g-o-s-p-e-l. When I hear it in the preaching, I see the g-o-s-p-e-l. When I see it in the love of my husband, my children, my friends, I see the g-o-s-p-e-l.

Because God loves us, "His divine power has granted to us all things that pertain to life and godliness, through the knowledge of him who called us to his own glory and excellence" (2 Pet. 1:3) It is simply and powerfully the g-o-s-p-e-l, a true miracle given by an amazing Savior, Brother, Priest, and King.

Jody Hogan

ACKNOWLEDGMENTS

During a conversation I recently engaged in with a friend who was inquiring about my writing, I said something like, "This message will be the only message I'll ever have from now on. This is it for me." She replied, "What a blessing that God has brought together so many threads of your life to this one convergence." I agreed.

There are so many threads that have converged in my heart; please allow me to say "thank you" to some of you for being the means the Lord used:

To Iain and Barbara Duguid for prying open my eyes to the gospel I thought I knew. To pastor Tim Keller who opened their eyes and through his Bible studies opened mine as well. To pastor John Piper for opening my eyes to the supremacy of God in all things.

To Craig Cabaniss, my first pastor at Grace Church, who taught me about first love without ever mentioning it.

To the leadership team at Sovereign Grace Ministries for humbly planting a church where I would be retaught to say the Name.

To Steve and Vikki Cook and the rest of the musicians who write the gospel-centered music for SGM that warms my affections and informs my soul.

To Al Fisher and Lydia Brownback at Crossway who so enthusiastically welcomed me in and understood right away what I meant when I said that I wanted to write a book about the gospel for believers.

To Paul David Tripp for talking and writing about the Redeemer, and for sharing with me his wisdom about identity.

To my friends at Grace Church who loved me, prayed for me, excused me from the duty I owed them, drew me out, and challenged me, and especially to our small group: Dana and Phil, Laura and Bingo, Donna, Laura L., Bev, Dave and JoLyn, Mike and Beth, Frank and Karolyn, Brian and Jody, Robert and Lynette, Rich and Cherie; to our associate pastors and their wives, Dan and Leslie, Eric and Kirsi.

To my dear pastor and his wife (my pal), Mark and Rondi Lauterbach, who live gospel-driven lives. Mark read every chapter and gave me immensely helpful insights, steering me away from heretical sloughs, encouraging me with humble insights. Much of what you now hold in your hands comes from his sermons.

To my dear family who have waited for me and especially to my grandchildren: Wesley, Hayden, Eowyn, Allie, Gabriel, and Colin, who didn't get to spend much time with their Mimi this past year because I was busy writing.

To my dearest husband, Phil, who once so gently stated, "You know, it's my house, too," when I was irritated that his arrival at home interrupted my thought. Thank you, my love. Whatever fruit our Lord might bring from this belongs to you and grew from your faithful prayer, gentle leadership, loving encouragement, and enduring patience.

And finally, to Jesus Christ, the One I said I loved but rarely thought about until he reminded me, "You know, it really is all about me." I am blessed.

The "Must-Read"
Introduction:
Are You Forgetting Something?

Have you ever had that uncomfortable feeling that you've forgotten something important but just can't remember what it is? I had that experience a few weeks ago as my husband and I were leaving church on Sunday morning. I had a niggling sense that I was forgetting something but I just couldn't pinpoint what it was. Purse? Nope. Bible? Got it. Then, as we proceeded down the main street toward the freeway, suddenly I started yelling, "The boys, the boys, we've forgotten the boys!" As you can imagine, my husband instantly whipped the car around and raced back to the church. I jumped out and ran to find them. I had forgotten that my daughter had asked me to take our grandsons home with us, and when she heard how we almost left them, I'm sure it made her think twice about asking us again. I suppose that's something most of you can relate to, isn't it? We all know what it's like to unintentionally forget someone we love.

In Luke's Gospel, we read a similar story. Having completed their annual pilgrimage to celebrate the Passover in Jerusalem, Mary and Joseph set out to return to Nazareth. After they had gone a day's journey, they began to search for their son among relatives and acquaintances. Although they had presumed that he was somewhere in the group, they soon discovered that he was nowhere to be found. They returned to Jerusalem immediately and, after searching frantically for him for three days, they found him in the temple, in dialog with the teachers (Luke 2:41–45).

It seems to me that in some ways we're like Jesus' parents. Let me explain what I mean. By definition, we Christians joyously celebrate our Passover Lamb, our salvation with Jesus, but then, like his parents, we eagerly head on back to Nazareth, back to living out our beliefs *without a conscious awareness or acknowledgment of his presence*. Of course, we assume that he is somewhere nearby. We haven't felt his absence because we're so preoccupied with living life for him.

Please don't misunderstand. I'm not saying that he has left us behind. No, he has promised never to do that. What I am saying is that once we've been saved, once we've understood and accepted the message of the gospel, the person and work of the Redeemer becomes secondary to what we're focused on—living the Christian life. We love to remember him at Christmas and Easter. We adore him as the baby in the manger; we rejoice over the empty tomb. But aside from these two seasons, our attention is primarily focused on us, on our performance, on our spiritual growth. We know that the incarnation and resurrection are important truths to our initial salvation, but that's pretty much where their impact ends.

Let me illustrate what I mean. If I asked you, "Where did the ongoing incarnation of Jesus Christ intersect with your life yesterday?" would you have an answer? We all know that the crucifixion is important for our initial salvation, but what did it mean to you this morning? Does Calvary inform and warm your heart when you're waiting in line at the grocery store or hearing bad news from your doctor? Does his sinless life comfort you when you realize that you've just sinned in that same way *again*? In other words, *is he significantly relevant to you in your daily walk with him?*

I don't assume any malice toward him on our part in our virtual desertion of the Redeemer. Instead, I think the problem is that the answer to the question, Is Jesus relevant? is probably something like, "I guess he should be, but I don't see how." I think that we move past him because we don't really understand how God's love to us in the gospel applies to our lives practically, here on this side of Calvary. Yes, of course we know that he died for our sins and rose again, but what does that have to do with living life here in the twenty-first century? Again, how relevant is the gospel, the work of Jesus Christ, to you?

Perhaps another facet of our desertion of the Savior, and a more insidious one, is that, although all orthodox believers view salvation as his work, we believe that living the Christian life is solely ours. Yes, salvation is a wonderful gift, we think, but Christian living is where we've got to concentrate now.

I believe that most Christians think fondly of Jesus, are sincerely grateful for salvation, and remember his name as a tagline when they pray, but they don't see his work and life as something to contemplate every moment of every day. I have to admit that until fairly recently I, too, pursued godliness without much thought of him. Among those who would classify themselves as serious Christians, who study the Bible and want to please God, my guess is that the thought of revisiting the gospel seems like a step back into kindergarten. To put it another way, if I told you that this is a book about the gospel, would you automatically assume that it's for unbelievers?

What I'll be asking you to consider throughout this book may be summarized in one simple question: *In your pursuit of godliness, have you left Jesus behind?* Since this might be a new question for you, let me ask you a few more that will help clarify the answer.

• If I said that we're going to spend page after page considering God's love, would you feel the need to stifle a yawn? What does his transforming love mean to you today?

• Are you more focused on your performance for him or his for you?

• At the end of the day is there a rest in your soul because of him, or is there guilt and a determination that tomorrow you're going to "do better"?

• Do you still feel the need to prove that you're not "all that bad"? Do you get angry when people criticize or ignore you?

• You know that Jesus is the Door. Do you see how he is your life? Could you tell me exactly how he has transformed your daily life?

As we work through the answers to these questions together, I want you to be encouraged. This is an endeavor that your Savior is passionate about. His great accomplishments, so personally costly to him, are not to be relegated to some introductory course that gets stored in the garage with old yearbooks. No, they're to be constantly mused on and relentlessly rejoiced in by all who know them.

So let's ask him to enlighten us now as we embark upon our journey back to Jerusalem, searching for the Beloved Son. Unlike his parents, we won't have to search frantically. No, he is joyfully and patiently waiting to reacquaint you with his love and to make his undiminished presence the most relevant aspect of your life. Let's spend time thinking about our Savior and how what he has already done is meant to be the most significant characteristic of our faith and life for him.

PART ONE

How God's Love
Transforms Our Identity

CHAPTER ONE

REMEMBERING HIS LOVE

For God so loved the world, that he gave his only Son.

JOHN 3:16

I t's vital that you know where we're going in this book before
you begin, so in case you skipped the introduction, please take a
moment to go back to it. Thanks!

In this chapter we're going to look at God's love as seen in
the gospel, and then we'll consider why it is important for us to
remember it. I know that you probably think you've heard all of
this before. Let me assure you, it's my assumption that you have. I
know this good news won't be *new* news for many of you. Even so,
please let me beg your indulgence while we traverse this well-worn
highway again, in search of our Savior.

WHAT IS GOD'S LOVE AND WHY SHOULD I CARE?

When Forrest Gump humbly proclaimed, "I'm not a smart man, but
I know what love is," in a way he spoke for us all, didn't he? We all
think we know what love is. Each of us has our own definitions of
love, no matter how naïve or sophisticated we are.

Although we might have some conflicting definitions, this book
will remind you what *real* love looks like—love that has given
sacrificially, transforms powerfully, and lasts eternally. Simply put,
real love was profoundly and perfectly personified in Jesus Christ,
the God-Man who assumed human flesh, lived a perfect life, was
executed on a Roman cross, rose from the dead, and then ascended

to heaven, still embodied in human flesh, to pave the way for each of us. Real love is personified in the gospel, and living in its light is utterly essential for our transformation.

> Unacquaintedness with our mercies [and] our privileges . . . makes us go heavily, when we might rejoice; and to be weak, where we might be strong in the Lord. . . . *This is the will of God, that he may always be eyed as benign, kind, tender, loving, and unchangeable. Let, then, this be the saints' first notion of the Father—as one full of eternal, free love towards them.*[1]

It's essential for us to think about God's love today because it is only his love that can grant us the *joy* that will strengthen our hearts, the *courage* that will embolden us in our fight against sin, and the *assurance* that will enable us to open up our lives to him so that he might deal powerfully with our unbelief and idolatry. If we're not completely convinced that his love is *ours right now*— fully and unalterably ours—we'll always hide in the shadows, focusing on our performance, fearing his wrath. Prayer will be hard because we won't want to approach him or be transparent before him. Witnessing will be a chore, for who would want to talk to others about a god who is demanding, angry, or cold? If we don't consciously live in the light of his love, the gospel will be secondary, virtually meaningless, and Jesus Christ will fade into insignificance. Our faith will become all about us, our performance, and how we think we're doing, and our transformation will be hindered.

What must we remember? Simply that God loves us so much that he crushed his Son so that we might be his and that this love isn't based on our worthiness or performance. His love doesn't fluctuate from day-to-day. It was settled the moment he set it upon you before the foundation of the world. God has spoken to us about his love and the gospel in John 3:16: "For God so loved the world, that he gave his only Son, that whoever believes in him should not perish but have eternal life." Will that love transform the way you live today? It's meant to, but exactly how?

24

THE GOSPEL . . . AGAIN?

I realize that you might be thinking, "Oh yes, God's love, Jesus and the gospel . . . yes, yes, I know all about that. It's true that I love that story, and it's good to remember it so that I can tell it to my unsaved friends, but frankly, isn't that just a little elementary now that I'm saved? I mean, the gospel is great for those beginning the Christian life, but I think I've grasped it already. After all, I am a Christian! Are you saying that there's something more here I need to consider?" Yes, in fact I'm saying that if you neglect to focus on God's love for you in Christ, your Christianity will soon be reduced to a program of self-improvement—just one of many methods to help you "get your act together." And although that might seem like a worthy goal, it isn't true Christianity at all. True Christianity is not a program of self-improvement; it's an acknowledgment that something more than self-improvement is needed. What's needed is *death* and *resurrection:* gospel words, gospel constructs, gospel motives, gospel power—a loving Redeemer.

To illustrate what I mean about our need to remember God's love for us in the gospel, I've written out a very significant number of verses that encapsulate this message. Because I assume that you're already pretty familiar with these passages, their context, and what they signify, I'm not going to explain them. Instead, I'll let them speak directly to you. So please fight the temptation to skim over them because you think you already know about them. Instead, please ask the Spirit to make them live to you again.

> Blessed be the God and Father of our Lord Jesus Christ, who has blessed us in Christ with every spiritual blessing in the heavenly places, even as he chose us in him before the foundation of the world, that we should be holy and blameless before him. In love he predestined us for adoption as sons through Jesus Christ, according to the purpose of his will, to the praise of his glorious grace, with which he has blessed us in the Beloved. (Eph. 1:3–6)

> By the one man's disobedience the many were made sinners. (Rom. 5:19)

For there is no distinction; . . . all have sinned and fall short of the glory of God. (Rom. 3:22–23)

In you all the families of the earth shall be blessed. (Gen. 12:3)

Christ Jesus, who, though he was in the form of God, did not count equality with God a thing to be grasped . . . [was] born in the likeness of men. (Phil. 2:5–7)

Her offspring . . . shall bruise your head, and you shall bruise his heel. (Gen. 3:15)

"Greetings, O favored one, the Lord is with you!" (Luke 1:28)

"Do not be afraid, Mary, for you have found favor with God. And behold, you will conceive in your womb and bear a son, and you shall call his name Jesus. He will be great and will be called the Son of the Most High." (Luke 1:30–32)

The time came for her to give birth. And she gave birth to her firstborn son and wrapped him in swaddling cloths and laid him in a manger, because there was no place for them in the inn. (Luke 2:6–7)

"Fear not, for behold, I bring you good news of a great joy that will be for all the people. For unto you is born this day . . . a Savior, who is Christ the Lord." (Luke 2:10–11)

So by the one man's obedience the many will be made righteous. (Rom. 5:19)

Finally he sent his son to them, saying, "They will respect my son." (Matt. 21:37)

For to us a child is born, to us a son is given; and the government shall be upon his shoulder, and his name shall be called Wonderful Counselor, Mighty God, Everlasting Father, Prince of Peace. (Isa. 9:6)

For he grew up before him like a young plant, and like a root out of dry ground; he had no form or majesty that we should look at him, and no beauty that we should desire him. (Isa. 53:2)

"You are my beloved Son; with you I am well pleased." (Luke 3:22)

Jesus, when he began his ministry, was about thirty years of age, being the son (as was supposed) of Joseph . . . the son of Adam, the son of God. (Luke 3:23, 38).

"The Spirit of the Lord is upon me, because he has anointed me to proclaim good news to the poor. He has sent me to proclaim liberty to the captives and recovering of sight to the blind, to set at liberty those who are oppressed, to proclaim the year of the Lord's favor." (Luke 4:18–19)

He was despised and rejected by men; a man of sorrows, and acquainted with grief; and as one from whom men hide their faces he was despised, and we esteemed him not. (Isa. 53:3)

He came to his own, and his own people did not receive him. (John 1:11)

He went about doing good and healing all who were oppressed by the devil. (Acts 10:38)

"And as Moses lifted up the serpent in the wilderness, so must the Son of Man be lifted up, that whoever believes in him may have eternal life." (John 3:14–15)

Behold, my servant shall act wisely; he shall be high and lifted up, and shall be exalted. (Isa. 52:13)

"You are the Christ, the Son of the living God. . . . Blessed are you. . . . For flesh and blood has not revealed this to you, but my Father." (Matt. 16:16–17)

"Have I been with you so long, and you still do not know me?" (John 14:9)

"Get behind me, Satan! You are a hindrance to me. For you are not setting your mind on the things of God, but on the things of man." (Matt. 16:23)

Jesus . . . made himself nothing, taking the form of a servant. (Phil. 2:5, 7)

He laid aside his outer garments, and taking a towel, tied it around his waist. Then he poured water into a basin and began to wash the disciples' feet and to wipe them with the towel that was wrapped around him. (John 13:4–5)

"One of you will betray me." (John 13:21)

"You will all fall away, for it is written, 'I will strike the shepherd, and the sheep will be scattered.'" (Mark 14:27)

"If I must die with you, I will not deny you." And they all said the same. (Mark 14:31)

"Let not your hearts be troubled." (John 14:1)

"My soul is very sorrowful, even to death; remain here, and watch with me." (Matt. 26:38)

And . . . he fell on his face and prayed, saying, "My Father, if it be possible, let this cup pass from me; nevertheless, not as I will, but as you will." (Matt. 26:39)

"So, could you not watch with me one hour?" (Matt. 26:40)

"My Father, if this cannot pass unless I drink it, your will be done." (Matt. 26:42)

He . . . found them sleeping, for their eyes were heavy. (Matt. 26:43)

"See, the hour is at hand, and the Son of Man is betrayed into the hands of sinners." (Matt. 26:45)

"Would you betray the Son of Man with a kiss?" (Luke 22:48)

"Awake, O sword, against my shepherd, against the man who stands next to me. . . . Strike the shepherd, and the sheep will be scattered." (Zech. 13:7)

And they all left him and fled. (Mark 14:50)

He who did not spare his own Son but gave him up for us all, how will he not also with him graciously give us all things? (Rom. 8:32)

Now the chief priests and the whole Council were seeking testimony against Jesus to put him to death, but they found none. (Mark 14:55)

"Are you the Christ, the Son of the Blessed?"
"I am."(Mark 14:61–62)

"You also are not one of this man's disciples, are you?"
"I am not." (John 18:17)

"This is the heir. Come, let us kill him and have his inheritance." (Matt. 21:38)

"What further witnesses do we need? You have heard his blasphemy. What is your decision?" And they all condemned him as deserving death. And some began to spit on him and to cover his face and to strike him, saying to him, "Prophesy!" And the guards received him with blows. (Mark 14:63–65)

His appearance was so marred, beyond human semblance, and his form beyond that of the children of mankind. (Isa. 52:14)

"You say that I am a king. For this purpose I was born and for this purpose I have come into the world." (John 18:37)

And the soldiers led him away inside the palace . . . and they called together the whole battalion. And they clothed him in a purple cloak, and twisting together a crown of thorns, they put it on him. And they began to salute him, "Hail, King of the Jews!" And they were striking his head with a reed and spitting on him and kneeling down in homage to him. (Mark 15:16–19)

So Jesus came out, wearing the crown of thorns and the purple robe. Pilate said to them, "Behold the man!" (John 19:4–6)

"Behold your King!" (John 19:14)

"Away with him, away with him, crucify him!"

"Shall I crucify your King?"

"We have no king but Caesar."

So he delivered him over to them to be crucified. (John 19:15–16)

And when they had mocked him, they stripped him of the purple cloak and put his own clothes on him. And they led him out to crucify him. (Mark 15:20)

So they took Jesus, and he went out, bearing his own cross, to the place called The Place of a Skull. . . . There they crucified him. (John 19:16–18)

Surely he has borne our griefs and carried our sorrows; yet we esteemed him stricken, smitten by God, and afflicted. But he was wounded for our transgressions; he was crushed for our iniquities; upon him was the chastisement that brought us peace, and with his stripes we are healed. All we like sheep have gone astray; we have turned—every one—to his own way; and the LORD has laid on him the iniquity of us all. (Isa. 53:4–6)

"Truly, I say to you, today you will be with me in Paradise." (Luke 23:43)

He was oppressed, and he was afflicted, yet he opened not his mouth; like a lamb that is led to the slaughter, and like a sheep that before its shearers is silent, so he opened not his mouth. By oppression and judgment he was taken away . . . who considered that he was cut off out of the land of the living, stricken for the transgression of my people? . . . Yet it was the will of the LORD to crush him; he has put him to grief. (Isa. 53:7–8, 10)

"Woman, behold, your son!" (John 19:26)

"My God, my God, why have you forsaken me?" (Matt. 27:46)

"I thirst." (John 19:28)

"Father, into your hands I commit my spirit!" (Luke 23:46)

"It is finished." (John 19:28–30)

Now . . . we have died with Christ. (Rom. 6:8)

"Truly this man was the Son of God!" (Mark 15:39)

But one of the soldiers pierced his side with a spear, and at once there came out blood and water. (John 19:34)

In him we have redemption through his blood, the forgiveness of our trespasses, according to the riches of his grace, which he lavished upon us. (Eph. 1:7–8)

He humbled himself by becoming obedient to the point of death, even death on a cross. (Phil. 2:8)

It is God who justifies. (Rom. 8:33)

"Blessed are those whose lawless deeds are forgiven, and whose sins are covered; blessed is the man against whom the Lord will not count his sin." (Rom. 4:7–8)

"Certainly this man was innocent!" (Luke 23:47)

For our sake he made him to be sin who knew no sin, so that in him we might become the righteousness of God. (2 Cor. 5:21)

For while we were still weak, at the right time Christ died for the ungodly. . . . But God shows his love for us in that while we were still sinners, Christ died for us. Since, therefore, we have now been justified by his blood, much more shall we be saved by him from the wrath of God. For if while we were enemies we were reconciled to God by the death of his Son, much more, now that we are reconciled, shall we be saved by his life. (Rom. 5:6, 8–10)

And Joseph took the body and wrapped it in a clean linen shroud and laid it in his own new tomb, which he had cut in the rock. And he rolled a great stone to the entrance of the tomb and went away. (Matt. 27:59–60)

And they made his grave . . . with a rich man in his death. (Isa. 53:9)

For you have died, and your life is hidden with Christ in God. (Col. 3:3)

"Do not be alarmed. You seek Jesus of Nazareth, who was crucified. He has risen; he is not here." (Mark 16:6)

And you were dead in the trespasses and sins. . . . But God, being rich in mercy, because of the great love with which he loved us, even when we were dead in our trespasses, made us alive together with Christ. (Eph. 2:1, 4–5)

We believe that we will also live with him. We know that Christ, being raised from the dead, will never die again; death no longer has dominion over him. . . . The life he lives he lives to God. (Rom 6:8–10)

"Woman, why are you weeping? Whom are you seeking?" (John 20:15)

There is therefore now no condemnation for those who are in Christ Jesus. (Rom. 8:1)

"Mary . . ." (John 20:16)

Who shall separate us from the love of Christ? . . . For I am sure that neither death nor life, nor angels nor rulers, nor things present nor things to come, nor powers, nor height nor depth, nor anything else in all creation, will be able to separate us from the love of God in Christ Jesus our Lord. (Rom. 8:35, 38–39)

"Rabboni!" (John 20:16)

"I will never believe." (John 20:25)

Christ died for our sins. (1 Cor. 15:3)

"Peace be with you." (John 20:26)

Was buried . . . (1 Cor. 15:4)

"Do not disbelieve, but believe." (John 20:27)

Was raised . . . (1 Cor. 15:4)

"My Lord and my God!" (John 20:28)

He appeared . . . (1 Cor. 15:5)

"Blessed are those who have not seen and yet have believed." (John 20:29)

And when he had said these things, as they were looking on, he was lifted up, and a cloud took him out of their sight. (Acts 1:9)

Christ Jesus is the one who died—more than that, who was raised—who is at the right hand of God, who indeed is interceding for us. (Rom. 8:34)

We have an advocate with the Father, Jesus Christ the righteous. (1 John 2:1)

Christ is . . . seated at the right hand of God. (Col. 3:1)

. . . and raised us up with him and seated us with him in the heavenly places in Christ Jesus, so that . . . he might show the immeasurable riches of his grace in kindness toward us in Christ Jesus. (Eph. 2:6–7)

For you did not receive the spirit of slavery to fall back into fear, but you have received the Spirit of adoption as sons, by whom we cry, "Abba! Father!" (Rom. 8:15)

Therefore God has highly exalted him and bestowed on him the name that is above every name, so that at the name of Jesus every knee should bow, in heaven and on earth and under the earth, and every tongue confess that Jesus Christ is Lord, to the glory of God the Father. (Phil. 2:9–11)

And those whom he predestined he also called, and those whom he called he also justified, and those whom he justified he also glorified. (Rom. 8:30)

"The kingdom of the world has become the kingdom of our Lord and of his Christ, and he shall reign forever and ever." (Rev. 11:15)

Then I saw heaven opened, and behold, a white horse! The one sitting on it is called Faithful and True, and in righteousness he judges and makes war. His eyes are like a flame of fire, and on his head are many diadems, and he has a name written that no one knows but himself. He is clothed in a robe dipped in blood, and the name by which he is called is The Word of God. (Rev. 19:11–13)

When Christ who is your life appears, then you also will appear with him in glory. (Col. 3:4)

Then the angel showed me the river of the water of life, bright as crystal, flowing from the throne of God and of the Lamb. . . . No longer will there be anything accursed, but the throne of God and of the Lamb will be in it, and his servants will worship him. They will see his face, and his name will be on their foreheads. And night will be no more. They will need no light of lamp or sun, for the Lord God will be their light, and they will reign forever and ever. (Rev. 22:1, 3–5)

If God is for us, who can be against us? . . . Who shall bring any charge against God's elect? (Rom. 8:31, 33)

When his soul makes an offering for guilt, he shall see his offspring; he shall prolong his days; the will of the LORD shall prosper in his hand. Out of the anguish of his soul he shall see and be satisfied; by his knowledge shall the righteous one, my servant, make many to be accounted righteous, and he shall bear their iniquities. Therefore I will divide him a portion with the many, and he shall divide the spoil with the strong, because he poured out his soul to death and was numbered with the transgressors; yet he bore the sin of many, and makes intercession for the transgressors. (Isa. 53:10–12)

In him we have obtained an inheritance, having been predestined according to the purpose of him who works all things according to the counsel of his will, so that we who . . . hope in Christ might be to the praise of his glory. In him you also, when you heard the word of truth, the gospel of your salvation, and believed in him, were sealed with the promised Holy Spirit, who is the guarantee of our inheritance until we acquire possession of it, to the praise of his glory. (Eph. 1:11–14)

For this reason I bow my knees before the Father . . . that you, being rooted and grounded in love, may have strength to comprehend with all the saints what is the breadth and length and height and depth, and to know the love of Christ that surpasses knowledge, that you may be filled with all the fullness of God. (Eph. 3:14, 17–19)

In this the love of God was made manifest among us, that God sent his only Son into the world, so that we might live through him. In this is love, not that we have loved God but that he loved us and sent his Son to be the propitiation for our sins. (1 John 4:9–10)

When all things are subjected to him, then the Son himself will also be subjected to him who put all things in subjection under him, that God may be all in all. (1 Cor. 15:28)

To him be glory in the church and in Christ Jesus throughout all generations, forever and ever. Amen. (Eph. 3:21)

Time for a Heart Check

Please stop now for a moment of reflection. What did you think as you read the preceding verses? Allow me to suggest some possibilities:

• *Yada, yada, yada.* I've heard this a thousand times, maybe not just like that but a thousand times anyway. I need something new, perhaps a few concrete steps to help me change, not this same-old, same-old. . . . I know it should transform me, but I don't see how.

• *Oh dear, not again!* I know that I should be responding with some sort of gratitude because of God's love for me, but I already feel too guilty. This story doesn't remind me of his love for me, only of the way I fail to love him. Frankly, this story terrifies me.

• *That reminds me* . . . I know that there was a time when that story moved my heart and made me thankful, but that hasn't happened in a long time. I'm really going to get my act together now. Really.

- *I'm different from other people.* There was a time when that story meant something to me but I've had a hard life. I guess I know that Jesus loves me, but I need someone with real arms to hug me and stop the pain. God's love is nice, but it just isn't tangible enough for me now.

- *I've tried to live the life I know God wants me to live, but I just can't.* I really don't see how that story about God's love in Christ intersects with my struggle with worry [or gambling, gluttony, pornography, pride, anger, or gossip]. I'm looking for something that will make me better so that I can stop hurting people and live a productive, healthy life.

- *Sorry, too busy to read. Can you text-message me? Gotta run!*

Where did you find yourself in those responses? I'll admit that sometimes it's hard for me to connect the dots between God's love and my daily life. I continually strive and frequently fail to see how his love in Christ is all that I need and to understand how to live with the gospel motivating and informing every decision, every action, every word.

If you found yourself in any of the statements above, don't worry. Unless we're very intentional about meditating on these truths, they slip from our thoughts like misty dreams that evaporate in the morning light. That's why Luther said we must "take heed, then, to embrace . . . the love and kindness of God. . . . [and to] daily exercise [our] faith therein, entertain no doubt of God's love and kindness."[2]

I've written this book because grasping the reality of God's love will provide every answer to every question we have about him and ourselves. It will tell us who we are, why we're here, and how we're supposed to do what we're supposed to be doing. Delighting in God's love will transform everything about us, including who we are, or our identity. This love is illustrated for us in Scripture, and particularly in the story we call "the gospel."

Oh, here's one more item you'll need to know. I'll be using the term *gospel* very frequently in this book, so I want to define what I mean here. The gospel was summarized in the verses above. It is the incarnation, sinless life, substitutionary death, burial, bodily resurrection, ascension, and eternal reign of the Son of God, Jesus Christ. I'm going to be using the term *gospel* as shorthand for all those truths, and I'll also be helping you see how they are meant to tangibly impact every facet of your life today.

So now that you've gotten a taste of where we're going, let me give you a personal word of encouragement. If you're in Christ today, God's promise of relationship and identity with him is rooted in his ageless love: *I have loved you so much that I sent my Beloved Son to bring you to myself, that in believing this you might have eternal relationship with me. I will be your God, you will be my child. Rest and rejoice in all my love has done to transform you.* If, on the other hand, you're not sure you're a Christian, won't you please turn to the appendix right away? That way you'll know what I mean when I talk about God's love for us in Christ and what our response needs to be. Thank you!

In chapter 2, we'll start our discussion about God's astounding love with an initial look at who we are and how his love shapes what we'll call "our identity." For now, though, here's a reminder to us about the depth of his love for us: "In this is love, not that we have loved God but that he loved us and sent his Son to be the propitiation [the one who bears and takes away his wrath] for our sins" (1 John 4:10). Who are we? We are people who are being transformed by his love.

REALIZING HOW GOD'S LOVE TRANSFORMS YOUR IDENTITY AND LIFE

At the end of each chapter, you'll find questions to challenge you. I'll also suggest further Bible reading aimed at helping you understand the truths presented. Please plan to take the time to do this practical work, as the point of this book is not mere information but the transformation of your heart and life. These practical exercises will help you as you cooperate with the Spirit's purpose in this pursuit. You might also gather together with a friend or two to go through this study and the questions.

1) Do you have any hopes or expectations as you begin this study?

2) What is your response to the statement "If we're not completely convinced that his love is *ours, right now, fully and unalterably ours,* we'll always hide in the shadows, be focused on our performance, fearing his wrath"? Do you agree or disagree? How often do you think about God's love for you as demonstrated in the gospel? Do you just assume it?

3) Quote John 3:16. Does it inform your daily walk?

4) My premise for this book is that many of us are so focused on living the Christian life, we've left Jesus behind. Do you agree or disagree? Interact with that statement.

5) Summarize in four or five sentences what you've learned from this chapter.

CHAPTER TWO

IDENTITY AMNESIA

For this very reason, make every effort to supplement your faith. . . .
For whoever lacks these qualities is so nearsighted that he is blind,
having forgotten that he was cleansed from his former sins.

2 PETER 1:5, 9

Prior to his death in 1963, Pastor A. W. Tozer preached a series of sermons calling his church to embrace a more God-centered worship. In his fourth message he broached an unusual topic:

> One of the greatest tragedies that we find, even in this most enlightened of all ages, is the utter failure of millions of men and women ever to discover why they were born.
>
> Deny it if you will—and some persons will—but wherever there are humans in this world, there are people who are suffering from a hopeless and depressing kind of amnesia. It forces them to cry out, either silently within themselves or often with audible frustration, "I don't even know why I was born!"[1]

Let's continue our time remembering God's love for us in the gospel by considering a condition I'm calling "Identity Amnesia."[2] Although this diagnosis is seldom heard, I believe that Identity Amnesia is an epidemic in our churches, and it's easily diagnosed once you know the symptoms. This epidemic is seen in serious Christian books that focus on improving outer behaviors such as communication skills or self-discipline, or on even overcoming sin, without much reference to God's love for us or his ongoing work in us. It's seen in the hymns and choruses we sing in which we declare our determination to follow Christ without a mention of his determination to cause us to do so. It can be observed in the astounding absence of any reference to the gospel in sermons (aside from invitations to unbelievers).[3] These calls to godly living are built like houses in the sky: fine looking edifices, but lacking the essential foundation.

Instead of starting with our obligations to the Lord (and I do believe we have them!), where so many books do, I'm beginning here, with our perspective of who we are—our "identity"—because God's love first transforms our hearts, then it changes our behaviors. He does transform our outer, more noticeable behavior (where we usually focus), but this transformation has its genesis in the renovation of the hidden inner person. Without the recognition of this prior and ongoing work of love, we won't have the courage or strength we'll need to fight sin the way he is calling us to. We won't have the faith to continue to say, "Yes, Lord," unless we're resting securely in the eternal yes he has spoken over us.

The Lord begins his transforming work in us by building an entirely new foundation upon which to construct our outer, more noticeable, behavior. It's this inner transformation of our identity, the reality of his making, remaking, and sustaining us in our inner person, that we frequently neglect when striving to live the Christian life. And it's in our inner person, in our identity, motives, affections, and trust, that the truths of the gospel are most critical.

In response to God's love for us, the Spirit refashions us, both inside and out. He makes us profoundly new. He changes everything about us, giving us new answers to the fundamental questions of life such as, who am I? and why was I born? These are essentially questions of identity, and I think too many of us are suffering from amnesia, even those of us who claim belief in the saving grace of Jesus Christ. Again, I'm sure that you would be able to answer these fundamental questions biblically: "Who am I? I'm a child of God!"; "Why was I born? To serve him!" My premise, though, is that even though we know these basic answers, we don't see how these answers actually connect with our daily lives.

But I Haven't Forgotten Who I Am!

Let me assure you that my assumption is that you do, in fact, remember all the pertinent information about who you are and perhaps even your place in God's world. When I assert that we've got amnesia, I don't mean that we are unable to answer basic questions. What I'm asserting is that too many of us are suffering from *spiritual amnesia*; an amnesia that has obscured our true identity as it's been defined by the gospel.

Let me give you a little more help. What I'm calling spiritual amnesia might best be understood in this way: *even though we believe the gospel, the occasions in which the gospel (the incarnation, sinless life, death, bodily resurrection, and ascension of the Son of God) actually intersect and powerfully affect our daily life are infrequent.* We assent to these precious truths of Scripture, but we frequently find ourselves living life like practical atheists—not much different from our unbelieving neighbors down the street—except that our garages are empty on Sunday morning. We forget who he is, what he has done; we don't know why it really matters. Because of this, we fail to remember who we are and how he has called us to live. We forget gospel truths about:

• our individuality: Who are we as individuals? What makes us unique? How can we know ourselves—the realities of who we really are? Should we even care? Why?

• our relationships: To whom do we belong? How can we know that we're not alone? Are we loved by anyone? Have we been welcomed?

• our purpose: What are we here to do? Why were we born? What gives our existence meaning?

• our permanence: How can we assure ourselves that there is more to life than a few short years that we spend "fidgeting until we die"?[4] Is there something more? Does what we do here, in this infinitesimal moment, really matter? Will it live on, is there an ultimate meaning to our life's story?

• our fallibility: Is there lasting assurance that our sins, weaknesses, and failures are forgiven? How can we comfort our hearts as we see our own hypocrisies, hatreds, and self-indulgences? How can we survive our own dishonesty as we proclaim our desire to love God and others while we shove them aside and jockey for position, comfort, and recognition?

So the first question that I want to put to you at this point is, do you know who you are? Here it is again: specifically, how has the gospel defined and shaped you? Most Christians know that the gospel should have something important to say about their daily lives, but aside from a basic understanding that they somehow belong to God and that heaven awaits them, they don't see the pertinence of the incarnation, the resurrection, or the ascension. Words like election, justification, redemption, reconciliation, propitiation, sanctification, and glorification probably do carry some meaning for most of us, but if we're being honest, they just don't seem to intersect with life as it's lived out with dirty diapers, hives, or hurricanes. Even though many of us love and believe the good news about Jesus Christ, we rarely take that news as personally as it's meant to be taken.

What Have You Been Drinking?

One very common form of physical amnesia is caused by the over-consumption of alcohol. When a person drinks to the point of drunkenness, he is liable to forget what he has done or even how he got home. In like manner, I think that most of us have spiritual amnesia because of what we've been drinking. I believe that we all have had such a deep draught from the fountains of worldly wisdom that it's quite common for us to forget how the truths we hear in church on Sunday morning apply to our daily lives. Yes, we assent to those truths, but because we've ingested so much of the philosophies of the world, the important connections that would inform our spiritual identity are never made. Instead, what is stored briefly in our short-term memory quickly drowns in the swirling morass of the ideas, beliefs, and desires gushing out from Vanity Fair where we live.

To help you understand what I mean, let me give you an

example. Let's imagine that you've just had the experience of hearing an inspiring sermon on John 3:16 and God's love for you in Christ. You heard about the need to embrace this magnificent love wholeheartedly, to which you applied a very hearty "amen!" Now, let's fast-forward to Sunday afternoon after the church clothes have come off, the garage door has been closed, and the whole family can be who they *really* are. Is it possible for you to see yourself being angry, consumed with self-pity, or worried because you discovered you weren't invited to *the* special party, your children spoke disrespectfully to you in front of the pastor, your favorite football team is losing, or you failed to set the oven and your dinner didn't cook properly while you were at church?

Most of us view God's love and the gospel as elementary topics meant to get us in the front door of faith, and they are that. But we've forgotten how these truths are also to transform us every moment of every day—when we're watching our favorite team lose, when the roast is still as raw as it was when we left for church, when we're tempted to believe that we're nothing more than unloved, disrespected, hungry losers.

If the scenario above is not too much of a stretch for you to imagine, then you're suffering from spiritual amnesia. This kind of disconnect between our stated beliefs—*my identity is that I'm one who's been loved immeasurably by God and am one with him*—and our practical beliefs—*my identity and self-worth are determined by whether I am popular, respected, a winner, and well-fed*—is alcohol-induced; it's caused by our willful consumption of the intoxicating "wisdoms" of the world. Rather than being inebriated with God's mercy, grace, and Spirit (Eph. 5:18), we're staggering around under the misconception that we really do need to love, accept, and respect ourselves to make it through the day. We're reeling from the belief that the most important factor in any given day is our success or comfort. Life has become "about" us and God's love in the gospel has taken a seat in the back of the bus, behind coveted invitations, the respect of friends, NFL championships, and full stomachs. We mistakenly think that these things are measures of God's love for us because we've forgotten about the Lamb who takes away sin.

It's in these ways (and millions of others like them) that we forget who we are: incalculably sinful men and women who are loved immeasurably by an infinitely holy God. We also forget how we are called to respond: in grateful obedience. We fail to respond in this way because we've forgotten the comfort of the gospel; we've been welcomed, purified, and made acceptable by God's direct and loving intervention, and we think we have to fight to get what we mistakenly believe we need. Everything that needed to be done for us has been done. We don't need to fight to gain his love and acceptance.

What Have You Forgotten and How Would You Know?

In Peter's second epistle he lists the character traits that mark a believer's life: faith, virtue, knowledge, self-control, steadfastness, godliness, brotherly affection, love. Then he makes an interesting statement. He writes that "whoever lacks these qualities is so nearsighted that he is blind, having forgotten that he was cleansed from his former sins" (2 Pet. 1:9).

Peter writes that one reason we don't grow in ordinary, grateful obedience as we should is that we've got amnesia; we've forgotten that we were cleansed from our sins. In other words, he is saying that ongoing failure in sanctification (the slow process of change into Christlikeness) is the direct result of failing to remember God's love for us in the gospel. If we lack the comfort and assurance that his love and cleansing are meant to supply, our failures will handcuff us to yesterday's sins, and we won't have faith or courage to fight against them, or the love for God that's meant to empower this war. Please don't miss the import of Peter's statement. *If we fail to remember our justification, redemption, and reconciliation, we'll struggle in our sanctification.*

If you look at your life and it seems as though your growth has been at a standstill, if you don't see that your faith, virtue, knowledge, self-control, steadfastness, godliness, brotherly affection, and love have grown in measurable ways, Peter says it's because you've forgotten the gospel: *Christ died to cleanse you from sin.* He says that you've become nearsighted; you can only see what's right in front of your face. A spiritual blindness has overtaken you so that you don't see your Savior standing right there before your eyes. For instance, how can our *faith* grow if all we see before us is our record of failure? If we don't apprehend God's love for us in the gospel, then the faith we need to fight against sin's allurements will be absent, and although we'll know that we should try to do better, we won't believe that we can truly change. We'll also doubt his love for us and wonder why he doesn't give us what we think we need. We'll feel as though we've been deserted in this battle; we won't see our Captain leading us on.

Our *virtue* or moral excellence will also grow in direct proportion to our appreciation of the fact that we've been cleansed, forgiven, and loved. These truths will empower our desire to make the gospel glorious before the eyes of a watching world. Our lights will shine! Why? Because we've been so loved by our heavenly Father that those things that used to "charm us most" are seen for the pathetic counterfeits that they are. We'll be men and women in love with our Savior.

We'll grow in our *knowledge* of and acquaintance with him because we won't be afraid to get near to him. In fact, studying and fellowshiping with him will become our delight because we've seen and experienced how delightful he is and how kind he has been to us. We'll know Jesus in his love, and that knowledge will make us strong, which is why Paul prayed that the Ephesians would be able to grasp the incomprehensible: how much they were loved by their Father (Eph. 3:18–19).

Self-control will come more easily because the idols that used to draw us away from him will have lost their power to entice. Remember, it doesn't take much self-control to compel loving obedience and service to one who has loved us so much that he has sacrificed his most precious relationship to make us his own. We'll begin to see him as being so wonderful that we'll love to make him smile.

Our *steadfastness* will grow as we rest in his steadfast love for us. Especially when we face trials and suffering, when we're most tempted to give up, we won't be blinded by our pain but will instead see him standing there faithfully before us with thorn-pierced brow, making intercession for us that our faith will not fail.

We'll want to be *godly* because we'll want to be like him; our desires will be transformed when our eyes are fixed on his godliness. Why would we want to offend the One who has loved us so much that he has, through his life and death, sacrificially cleansed us from sin?

We will experience *affection* for our brothers and sisters because we'll see them as people who've been loved in the same way that we have. Our ambition, selfishness, and impatience will be swallowed up in humble amazement that he has loved us so much and suffered for us and we'll gladly welcome and serve all those whom our Father loves (Rom. 15:7).

And finally, we'll *love* because we'll be aware that we've been loved. The kind of love to which God has called us is responsive in nature; we can't manufacture it on our own. We'll love God because he has first and marvelously loved us, and this love will overflow to others, as well (1 John 4:8–9). These gospel truths are not insignificant, something only for beginners. In fact Paul writes:

> Now I would remind you, brothers, of the gospel I preached to you, which you *received, in which you stand, and by which you are being saved.* . . . For I delivered to you as of *first importance* what I also received: that Christ died for our sins. (1 Cor. 15:1–3)

The gospel message—you have been cleansed from sin—is the pinnacle of God's loving work in the world, and just as it is this work that saves us, it is also this work that *transforms* and *sustains* us. The gospel is the message that must remain paramount throughout all our life. It must not be relegated to yesterday's news or tucked away with the faded photos of our first steps in Christ. Jesus' death cleanses us from sin, but it also guarantees our ultimate transformation into his image. This transformation occurs, Paul writes, while we gaze upon him, think about him, and muse on him as he has revealed himself to us in the gospel. "And we all, with unveiled face, *beholding the glory of the Lord, are being transformed* into the same image from one degree of glory to another" (2 Cor. 3:18). Behold his glory in the gospel and be transformed.

It's a Willful Amnesia

So then, why, if all this is true, do so many of us fail to embrace the gospel on a daily basis? Why have we forgotten the gospel? Are we simply innocents with poor memories? Perhaps for some of us the key to our amnesia does lie in a basic ignorance. Perhaps we've never really been taught that the gospel should continue to mean something to us now that we're saved. But even if that's the case, even if we've never heard this before, in our hearts there is also an unquenchable thirst for words and beliefs that reassure, flatter, and puff us up. Instead of humbly receiving the gracious love of our Father and depending daily on him, we want to believe that we really can improve ourselves. We want to approve of our record; we believe that if we just try hard enough, we'll finally be successful. God's love is wonderful at first blush, but because it's not based on anything we've done, it humbles us to the dust. In addition, we desire the approbation and accolades of our peers. So instead of embracing his love as our only comfort, our idolatrous hearts gravitate to the saloons of worldly wisdom, and we're inebriated before we know it. We might pause at the cross for a moment or two, but then we slink away, back to our old haunts where we can hear what we like to hear. The attitudes of the world—self-improvement, self-reliance, self-love, self-promotion, pride, independence, and self-worship—resonate within each of us and drown out our Redeemer's loving words.

It's so easy for us to completely forget who we are: sinners saved by grace—created in the image of God for his pleasure—weak and dependent creatures who must rely every moment of every day on his grace and mercy. We've got problems with spiritual amnesia because we've sung the world's song too many times, and *Rock of Ages* is, frankly, a bit out of style. *Why would I need to hide myself?* we wonder. We think that we don't need to hide ourselves in him; we just need to find the key to the successful Christian life in a better self-help book.

We're all living on this side of the fall, clothing ourselves with fig-leaf, false identities in a vain effort to make ourselves more presentable. We sew and sew, but just can't seem to get it right. So we give up sewing for a while, and then we begin all over again. We don't want people to see us as we are because we are both proud and ashamed; we're too proud to admit our sin; we're too ashamed to say we still need a Savior. We aren't seeing ourselves as we are. We've forgotten his love and the gospel and our true identity.

I WILL BE YOURS, YOU WILL BE MINE

Do you like to eat those little heart candies that you can find around Valentine's Day? I do—or, I should say, I used to. As you're munching away, every now and then, you'll come across one that reads, "Be Mine." Although God's love is certainly deeper than a sentiment on a little candy Valentine, this is one he has sent to you. He has not only asked you to be his, but he has taken you to himself. He has cleared away every obstacle that would thwart this relationship that means so much to him. God has made a pronouncement: "I will be your God; you will be my possession." When we consider who we are, we're to define ourselves by that decree alone. The wonderful news is *we are his*! But that isn't the best news of all. The really wonderful news is that he has given himself to us. *He is ours*! So, you see, you were right when you answered that first identity question, "Who are you?" with the answer, "A child of God!" but that's a truth that must be pressed into our consciousness every moment of every day. When dissed by our friends, when we're struggling with pain, when falling into sin (again!), we're still his children. And that's the most important thing about who we are.

God has graciously chosen, adopted, and sealed us for his own glory. He is giving himself to us, and if we're not distracted by our self-efforts and self-trust, we will respond by defining ourselves by that love. Who are you? You're his, he is yours, and you've been cleansed from sin. And that's all the identity any of us need.

I know that I've covered a lot of ground in this chapter and I also know that some of what I've said might have seemed new or uncomfortable for you. As we continue on in our study, you'll see how what we've discussed here has real-life consequences in your day-to-day walk with your Savior. I also want you to know that I trust that God will grant you a new appreciation of who you are in him. He is the one who has to give you the grace to overcome the spiritual amnesia that may be, even now, clouding your thoughts. Here's the truth about our dilemma: "We are blind to God unless he shines his light in our hearts. We are terrified of him unless he reveals his love. We are lost from him unless he makes a way."[5] But he has shared his light; he has revealed his love. He has given us the gospel.

God has already done everything that needs to be done for us in Christ. Through Jesus, he has lovingly revealed himself to us: "For God, who said, 'Let light shine out of darkness,' has shone in our hearts to give the light of the knowledge of the glory of God in the face of Jesus Christ" (2 Cor. 4:6). He has openly demonstrated his love: "But when the goodness and loving kindness of God our Savior appeared, he saved us" (Titus 3:4–5). He has also made the way for us to come to him and to know that we're his:

> Therefore, brothers, since we have confidence to enter the holy places by the blood of Jesus, by the new and living way that he opened . . . through his flesh . . . let us draw near with a true heart in full assurance of faith. (Heb. 10:19–22)

He has called to us, "Be Mine." If you're his child, he wants to assure you of his unchangeable love for you and your place in him even now. We can boldly respond to him in the full assurance that he really does love us, that he really has welcomed us to himself and made us his own. He loves for us to come to him and rely on him, just as a loving father loves to know that his children trust him and love to be with him.

If he is willing to open to you the holy places where his presence dwells through the blood of his Son, he'll also gently, patiently, and lovingly reveal all you need to know about who you are and more importantly, who he is. Rejoice, dear friend, in this amazing love and your completely new identity.

In order to facilitate further awareness of yourself and your God, please take time to complete the exercises below.

Realizing How God's Love Transforms Your Identity and Life

1) Define spiritual amnesia. Do you think you're suffering from it?

2) I wrote, "The attitudes of the world—self-improvement, self-reliance, self-love, self-promotion, pride, independence, and self-worship—resonate within each of us and drown out our Redeemer's loving words." Do you see these attitudes in yourself? Do you see them in your desire to grow in maturity in the Lord? Do you see how they play into your sins and failures?

3) How convinced are you that the key to transforming your identity and life lies in an ongoing appreciation of God's love as seen in the gospel story? What are your objections to this statement?

4) 2 Peter 1:9 reads, "For whoever lacks these qualities is so nearsighted that he is blind, having forgotten that he was cleansed from his former sins." When you look closely at your life, do you see that Christlike qualities are present and increasing? I know that it's really hard to judge yourself in this way (since some of us tend to be so hard on ourselves that we're blind to God's grace, and others are so easy on themselves that they think there's growth when there isn't!), so why not ask a longtime friend what he sees in your life? When you act in an un-Christlike manner, do you remind yourself of the gospel, that you've been loved and cleansed from former sins? Does this reminder push you toward holiness or into further sin?

5) Summarize in four or five sentences what you've learned from this chapter.

CHAPTER THREE

THE IDENTITY GIFT

When Christ who is your life appears, then you also will appear with him in glory.

COLOSSIANS 3:4

As much as I dislike commercials, I have to admit that from time to time, the folks on Madison Avenue do come up with some pretty amusing ones, like those identity theft warnings from Citibank. I especially enjoyed watching the one where the dowdy, older man speaks with the voice of a young Valley girl. "First, I emptied the checking account," she brags, "and then I hit the mall. And there, in the window, was this sexy little outfit, and oh, my gosh . . ."[1] Although this scenario was humorous to watch, it certainly wouldn't be much fun to live through, would it?

Just in case you're unaware, identity theft occurs when someone steals your name and other personal information for fraudulent use. Most of us are dismayed by this new cyber-age crime, and we wouldn't assume that the theft of another person's identity is acceptable behavior. The surprising reality, however, is that Christians are, by definition, people who have someone else's identity. They're called "Christians" because they've taken the identity of someone else: the Christ. Not only have you been given an identity that you weren't born with or that you didn't earn the right to use, but you're invited to empty the checking account and use all the benefits this identity brings! This is so much better than identity theft—it's an identity gift! Your new identity is encapsulated in a phrase from the verse we opened this chapter with: "Christ is . . . your life" (Col. 3:4).

The reason we're going to spend time talking about your new identity is that many of us function as though this gracious gift had never been given. We view our life as though our identity hadn't changed, instead of seeing with eyes of faith. Our answers to the fundamental questions about who we are, what we're doing, and where we're going are frequently no different from our unbelieving neighbor's. We're like the proverbial heiress who has millions in the bank but lives under a bridge begging for change to buy another bottle of wine. Yes, we know that we're called "Christian," but do we know what that means?

CHRIST IS OUR LIFE

As Christians we say we've been given Christ's identity; after all, we're "Christians"! We know that we are "in" him in some way and that we're part of God's family, but the way that we function in our day-to-day lives may say that we have forgotten who we really are. We recognize that we have Christ's identity, but because we have spiritual amnesia, we live as though it isn't what's most true about us.

For instance, when we impatiently await a tardy handyman, inhale exhaust fumes on an overcrowded freeway, or listen to our children insist for the umpteenth time that they *did* study for the spelling test, we may remember our true identity and respond in grace because we're convinced that Colossians 3:4 is true. Christ—not home repairs, clean air, or successful children—is our life. On the other hand, we might forget who we are and respond instead in self-righteousness, a craving for respectability, or even a faithless self-loathing. This *functional identity* might express itself in these ways.

• When I make an appointment, I keep it! If that repairman was going to be late *again*, the least he could do is call! I may not be perfect, but at least I'm more responsible than he is!

• You're going to do better on your spelling tests or I'm going to know the reason why! It's so embarrassing when you fail like this!

• I'm a failure! Here I am, stuck in this dead-end job, on this stupid freeway, going nowhere, sinning like I always have. I guess this is what I deserve. I'm such a loser.

How would these responses differ if we were remembering that because of God's love, Christ is our life? Perhaps the following suggestions will connect the realities of our new identity with the day-to-day trouble we face.

When it seems as though I've wasted an afternoon waiting for a repairman, I can temper my response in light of heavenly realities:

• Christ is overwhelmingly patient with me. His gracious patience with my irresponsibility is a truth that I need to be reminded of over and over again. The irresponsibility of this repairman is nothing in contrast to mine, and yet I've been chosen and loved by God, so I can be merciful and patient with others. Responding graciously to this repairman is not simply a decision of my will, but it is also a recognition of Jesus' gracious response to me.

When my children fail to perform in a way that shows off my parenting skills, I must remind myself that I don't deserve anyone's respect and my desire for it proves that.

• Christ has given me a new identity. The mere fact that Christ has had to give me his identity means that everything I have, including any respectability I might think I deserve, is not worth the effort I've expended to keep it. Why do I think I deserve anyone's respect? I am commanded to nurture and discipline my children *for God's glory*, not my own. When they fail, which of course they will— after all they're born in my likeness—I can comfort and instruct them because I'm a failure who's been comforted and instructed. Responding in kindness to their failures is not a simple matter of bootstrap obedience; it's a recognition of what the cross has declared about me and my identity. I've got a faithful heavenly Father who has adopted me, so I don't need to use my children to prove that I'm really okay. He has made me his own; that's all that matters.

When I find myself stuck in traffic on my way to what seems like a meaningless job, my identity in Christ will inform and transform the way that I think about myself and my day.

• I'm in union with him right now, in this car, on this freeway. Because he is with me, time spent in traffic is a joy because it's time spent with him. He has identified with my helpless plight, with my very person; he is beside me *now*. He knows what it is to work, and his perfect work record has been credited to me. My success and value aren't based on whether I have a well-paying job that others approve of or clear sailing on the road. In fact, I don't need to be concerned with these things at all, because I've been given assurances that eclipse all else. I've been given the God-Man, Jesus Christ, who is able to save me to the uttermost and who is living, right now, in this very instant, to make intercession for me before his Father (Heb. 7:25). I can persevere with hope because this car, job, freeway does not define me. Although it's true that I am sitting in this car, I'm also seated with Christ in heavenly places.

Again, Paul wrote:

> If then you have been raised with Christ, seek the things that are above, where Christ is, seated at the right hand of God. Set your minds on things that are above, not on things that are on earth. For you have died, and your life is hidden with Christ in God. When Christ who is your life appears, then you also will appear with him in glory. (Col. 3:1–4)

As you read over the passage above, what stood out to you? For most of us, the commands of the verse draw our attention: "Seek the things that are above. . . . Set your minds on the things above." Although these are significant commands, we rarely realize that most of the passage doesn't have anything to do with our work, but rather with his. Because we skip over the facts we think we already know, the transforming power that we need is absent.

Paul writes that because we're hidden with Christ in God and he is our life, we're to set our minds and desires on the things that are above, where we are *even now* seated with him (Col. 3:1).

When we fail to respond in Christlikeness to the disappointments of life, it's usually because we've forgotten all he has accomplished for us. We forget that the old person who lived for respect and demanded smooth sailing was crucified with him. He died, and a new person has been raised to life in his place. Just as Christ was made alive by the Spirit, so have we. Because we're now one with him in his resurrection life, raised by the same Spirit that raised him, the earthly things that used to drive us have lost their power. We've been given new eyes that provide us with the courage to see ourselves as we really are and the faith to believe that he really is recreating us to be like him. Paul speaks of us in both the "already" and the "not yet": we're as alive with him right now as we will ever be; we're seated with him in heaven, but this resurrection life is still confined to our mortal bodies, so we still have to consciously "seek" and "set."

This new identity is inalterably ours right now, but we've also got to grow into it, just as my grandchildren are growing in their understanding of what it means to be part of our family. Part of this maturing process is the ability to identify and put to death the self-centered motives that formerly earmarked our lives. So Paul goes on to tell us to walk in the compassion, kindness, humility, meekness, and patience that characterized Jesus' life. We can walk in this new life because through the Spirit he lives in us. We can bear with one another and forgive each other because he has forgiven us. "And above all these [we're to] put on love, which binds everything together in perfect harmony" (Col. 3:12–14).

Our problem is that if we don't continually remind ourselves of how he has chosen, renamed, and remade us, the struggle to grow in Christian character will become nothing more than another attempt at self-improvement, and self-improvement always results in self-loathing or pride.[2] Our Savior has declared that we are completely dependent upon him and what he accomplished for us, but in overconfidence we hastily run past his accomplishments and seek rest in our own.

Lucifer's Error

Augustine wrote that the error of Lucifer was that he wished *no other source of goodness than himself.* "He tried to be his own source and so he fell. This basic denial of dependence is what ruins us."[3] You see, the problem with attempting independently to construct our own identity is that the One who created us, who loves us and has the authority to name us, has already told us who we are, what we need, and where we're going. He has determined our individuality, our place of belonging, our purpose, and our permanence. He has answered our fallibility.

He has defined our *individuality* by calling us by name. "But now thus says the LORD, he who created you . . . he who formed you . . . 'Fear not, for I have redeemed you; I have called you by name, you are mine'" (Isa. 43:1). He has engraved our name on the palms of his hands (Isa. 49:16). He knows our heart and our thoughts (Psalm 139). You're not just one in millions, a face lost in the crowd. In the heart of God you're unique, a distinct person with a particular name, chosen from before the foundation of the world (Eph. 1:4).

He determined our *relationships* when he said, "I will take you to be my people, and I will be your God" (Ex. 6:7). He declared, "Behold, the dwelling place of God is with man. He will dwell with them, and they will be his people, and God himself will be with them as their God" (Rev. 21:3). Just as a man in love marries and bestows his name upon his bride, he has given us his. We don't have to wonder about his thoughts toward us: we're called by his name (Acts 15:17).

The purpose of our life is to reveal to others how wonderful he is and to glorify and enjoy him eternally. As the Westminster Divines asked and answered, "What is the chief end [purpose] of man? To glorify God and enjoy Him forever." These godly men were simply echoing Paul's thought in Romans 11:36: "For from him and through him and to him are all things. To him be glory forever." Why are you here? Why were you ever born? To glorify and enjoy him! The blessedness of this truth is found in the reality that he has loved us and is transforming us so that we do, even now, glorify him. The angels look at us—when we sin, when we forget him, when we obey out of love, when we obey out of pride and self-effort—and worship God for his great love and mercy. He is garnering worship to himself. The gospel makes him glorious!

The *permanence* of our person and work has been established by him, as well. We're going to live in his presence eternally (John 3:16), and our efforts at grateful and ordinary obedience make an eternal difference (John 15:16; 1 Cor. 3:14–15; 15:46). Because we've been loved by him, our lives are not in vain.

The problem of our ongoing fallibility and failure has been answered in the gospel. We are, each one, more sinful and flawed than we ever dared believe, but more loved and welcomed than we ever dared hope.[4] The love of God for us in the gospel assures our hearts and brings us peace, especially when we see our sins and failures.

We can rejoice because our basic identity questions have all been answered in him. Who we are as individuals, our place of belonging, the purpose of our lives, the permanence of our existence and work have all been answered forever. We are loved, welcomed, adopted, united to him, and forgiven. Nothing, not even our sin, will ever change what he has done.

The gospel tells us that our new identity is found in Christ alone. But we forget that we are sinful and flawed and don't deserve respect. We also forget that we've been loved and welcomed by the only Person whose opinion really matters. We've forgotten God's love for us in the gospel. Our fundamental problem is not our history, our environment, our brain chemicals, or even our bad choices. Our problem is that we've got a functional identity that flies in the face of gospel truth. We've ignored and disregarded the fact that Christ has given us his identity: he is our life.

The questions that occupy our hearts should not be why don't my kids respect me? Why do I have to wait for this stupid worker?

Why can't I get a better job? Why doesn't my spouse or children or parents or boss or friend appreciate me? The questions we should ask are: Why would God send his Son to die for me, his wretched enemy? (Rom. 5:8, 10); Why would he make him who knew no sin to be sin so that I might reap all the benefits of his righteousness? (2 Cor. 5:21); Why would I, who was dead in trespasses and corruption, who carried out every wicked desire of my body and mind and who was, by nature, a child of his wrath, be made alive together with Jesus? Why should I be a partaker of his never-dying life? Why am I not hanging on a cross? The only answer to these questions is that God, who is rich in mercy, *has loved us with his great love and showered us with his grace*! (Eph. 2:2–6). This is our identity!

In light of these gospel truths, the depth of God's love is staggering! The truth that many of us have lost and desperately need to find is that Christianity isn't essentially a program to help moral people be better. No, it's a relationship based on the premise that we aren't good now and will never be good enough in this life. We need someone to be good in our place, to suffer what we deserve to suffer, and to live the righteous life we should have lived. Our Redeemer has taken our sinful identity so that we might receive his righteous one! Can you see how it has to be Christ *alone* who defines everything we were, are, or ever will be? He is our life! He is our identity!

The Wonderful News

The gospel really is good news, isn't it? It's not simply that we've been saved from hell by a God who is tolerating us, keeping us at arm's length, granting us a salvation that didn't cost him much. He sent his "one and only" Son to die in our place that he might bring us to himself. That's how intent he was on transforming you. On the night he was betrayed, he prayed that we would know that we've been loved by the Father with the same intensity of love he has for his beloved Son (John 17:23).

Rather than defining ourselves as we used to, we've got to define ourselves according to the truths of the gospel. Who are we? We're women and men who are so sinful and flawed that we deserve hell, but we've been so loved and welcomed that every spiritual blessing, adoption, tender fellowship with our Father and each other, forgiveness, reconciliation, and eternal life is ours. Christ's accomplishments and perfections are ours now. Everything about us is different.

Our history has changed. We are no longer merely the children of our biological parents. We've been irrevocably adopted by our Father in heaven, and his story is now our story. We're part of the glorious unfolding of his plan and find our place in his purposes in the earth. Who are you? You are a child of your Father, the King who comforts your timorous heart so that when you are tempted and tried, you may confidently cry, "Abba, Father!" (Rom. 8:15; Gal. 4:5–7). Instead of having just one or two siblings, you are a member of his body, in communion with all our brothers and sisters from all ages (1 Cor. 12:12–13). You're a member of God's heavenly family; Paul, Peter, John, and even Jesus himself are your brothers. Mary, his earthly mother, is your sister. "Beloved we are God's children *now*" (1 John 3:2). In our new identity, we no longer identify ourselves by our nationality, gender, denomination, or economic status because "Christ is all, and in all" (Col. 3:11). This radical adoption tears down all the barriers that once separated brother and sister and makes us all one in him, "for in Christ Jesus you are all sons of God. . . . There is neither Jew nor Greek, there is neither slave nor free, there is neither male nor female, for you are all one in Christ Jesus" (Gal. 3:26, 28).

Our citizenship has changed. We are citizens of the City of God, "a chosen race, a royal priesthood, a holy nation, a people for his own possession." We have a new purpose in life, to "proclaim the excellencies of him who called us out of darkness into his marvelous light." Our new motive for godly living is that although once we were not "a people . . . now [we] are God's people"; once we hadn't "received mercy, but now we have received mercy" (1 Pet. 2:9–10).

Right now we're seated together with him at the right hand of our Father. Because Christ is our life, "our citizenship is in heaven, and from it we await a Savior, the Lord Jesus Christ" (Phil. 3:20).

Not only has our past and present identity changed, *our future has changed* as well. We're no longer indentured to the gods of this earth, striving to amass wealth, knowledge, respect, or friends. We're not enslaved to futility, seeking to fill meaningless hours with meaningless labor or overcome boredom through joyless pleasure until we finally die. No, now we're awaiting a Savior who will come to gather us from our exile. In the twinkling of an eye, Christ, who is our life, will appear, and then *we* will appear with him in glory.

> Our identifying way of life, our heartland . . . derive not from this world but from heaven. . . . This citizenship comes complete with a story of our origins and our destination: we live in the hope that one day our Savior will come riding out of the gates to gather his people from exile. Finding us and retrieving us, he will transform our mortal, decaying frames to be like his glorious resurrected and ascended body.[5]

Soon, we'll find ourselves transported into a city where there will never be any sin, loneliness, confusion, crying, or shame. Then we'll finally grasp the enormity of the statement, "Christ is our life." Because of this glorious future, our faith and work for him today are not in vain.

It is this new identity that must define and transform us today. Our life is no longer bound up in the vicissitudes of random daily chaos, even if the repairman is late, our children are poor spellers, or we're stuck behind a truck that's spewing diesel fumes into our car. We can, at last, dismantle our grinding quid-pro-quo *demandingness* and rest in the truth that we don't deserve mercy, but we've been declared not guilty in Christ. His love has swallowed up all our petty calls for fairness through his incarnation, life, death, resurrection, and ascension. Where is "fairness" in the gospel?

Our desire to be respected will end up where it belongs—on the ash heap with our pride—when we see that our former identity and reputation was utterly demolished on the cross. We've got nothing left to prove anymore; we deserve the death he died. We're sinners saved by grace alone; our children are sinners who will be saved by grace alone. It's his reputation, not ours, that matters.

The hours and hours we've wasted in pride and hedonistic self-recrimination—*I can't believe I did THAT again!*—will be transformed into humble thanksgiving for the One who perfectly fulfilled every law and whose perfect record and standing are now ours, all to the praise of his glorious grace.

To the Praise of His Glorious Grace

Now let me focus your attention where it rightfully belongs. When a friend gives a wonderful gift, it is right to examine and relish the gift. But it isn't right for the glory to remain on the gift itself, no matter how wonderful it may be. The focus belongs on the generosity of the giver. Our Father is the giver of this identity gift through the atoning sacrifice of the Son as it is applied by the Spirit. Simply speaking, he has done all he has done so that our lives would overflow with loving praise for his glorious grace (Eph. 1:6, 12, 14).

The gospel is good news for us, yes, but the goodness of this good news is not primarily us or even our new identity. It is good news about him: his mercy, his faithfulness, his holiness and atoning sacrifice. It's a report about his great condescension as he traded his glorious identity for our shameful one. It's about his flawless character and infinite compassion. Even though he has become our life, the emphasis belongs on him, not on our identity, our sin, our standing, our successes, or even our joys. As wonderful as the gift of an entirely new, clean identity is, we won't spend eternity rejoicing in it. We'll spend eternity rejoicing in him. We'll sing, "Worthy is the Lamb who was slain, to receive power and wealth and wisdom and might and honor and glory and blessing! . . ." This resounding chorus will fill our mouths as it fills all heaven: "To him who sits on the throne and to the Lamb be blessing and honor and glory and might forever and ever!" (Rev. 5:12–13). Jesus Christ, not any of us, no matter what we accomplish for him, will be the focus of the worship of heaven. *Christ* is our life now, and he'll remain our life in joyful praise forever.

Realizing How God's Love Transforms Your Identity and Life

1) Our definition of the good news is that we are so sinful and flawed that we deserve eternal punishment but that we are more loved and welcomed than we could ever hope. Think back over your day and try to identify where this gospel truth intersected with your life. Were you consistently aware that what you deserve has been replaced by what Christ has given? Were you aware of and thankful for this identity transfer?

2) What follows is a list of a few verses that will help you begin to construct a new identity. As you read each one, ask the Lord to help you see how it might apply to you.

• "He is the source of your life in Christ Jesus, whom God made our wisdom and righteousness and sanctification and redemption. Therefore, as it is written, 'Let the one who boasts, boast in the Lord.'" (1 Cor. 1:30–31)

• "And it is God who establishes us with you in Christ, and has anointed us, and who has also put his seal on us and given us his Spirit in our hearts as a guarantee." (2 Cor. 1:21–22)

• "Therefore, if anyone is in Christ, he is a new creation. The old has passed away; behold, the new has come." (2 Cor. 5:17)

• "For in Christ Jesus you are all sons of God." (Gal. 3:26)

• "I have been crucified with Christ. It is no longer I who live, but Christ who lives in me. And the life I now live in the flesh I live by faith in the Son of God, who loved me and gave himself for me." (Gal. 2:20)

• "[I may] . . . be found in him, not having a righteousness of my own that comes from the law, but that which comes through faith in Christ, the righteousness from God that depends on faith." (Phil. 3:9)

3) You were given your father's name when you were born. You've also been given your heavenly Father's name. What does it mean to have his name? What does it mean for you to bear the name "Christian"? See Isaiah 62:2–3; 43:1–7; Jeremiah 33:14–17; John 17:11–13, 26; and Revelation 3:12–13.

4) Blaise Pascal wrote, "Not only do we only know God through Jesus Christ, but we only know ourselves through Jesus Christ; we only know life and death through Jesus Christ. Apart from Jesus Christ we cannot know the meaning of our life or of our death, of God, or of ourselves."[6] What does Jesus Christ teach you about who you are and what your life ultimately means? What does he teach you about your heavenly Father?

5) Summarize in four or five sentences what you learned from this chapter.

CHAPTER FOUR

THE VERDICT

There is therefore now no condemnation for those who are in Christ Jesus.

ROMANS 8:1

I don't know how many of you will remember the heartbreaking murder of a seven-year-old girl here in San Diego, back in February 2002. Little Danielle van Dam was kidnapped from her bedroom during the night and murdered. Her body was then dumped in a field twenty-five miles from her home. I followed the investigation into her disappearance, the accumulation of evidence, the ultimate trial and sentencing of a neighbor, fifty-year-old David Westerfield, with grief. I talked with friends who lived in their neighborhood, got a sense of their opinion, and watched as the district attorney built his case. Would the evidence against Westerfield be solid enough to convict him? Was he truly guilty?

Once the verdict and sentence were read, everyone in Danielle's neighborhood was relieved to hear that Westerfield would never come back and that he would get what he deserved: death. Our community certainly would have been up in arms if he had gotten away with his crime or if the sentence handed down had been too lenient, especially in light of the heinousness of what he had done.

BUT THAT'S NOT FAIR!

Like you, I hate injustice. Our hatred of injustice is part of what it means to be created in the image of God. God's own testimony about himself is that he is just (Deut. 32:4; Isa. 30:18), and that he hates injustice: "He who justifies the wicked and he who condemns the righteous are both alike an abomination to the LORD" (Prov. 17:15). We're like him: we love justice and hate injustice. We want everything to be fair, and we want the bad guys to pay. We might not all agree about capital punishment, but everyone does agree that criminals should be punished in some way that approximates the pain they have inflicted upon others. On the other hand, we strongly object when those who are obviously innocent are condemned. Why, even the youngest child knows how to protest, "But, Mom, that's not fair!"

WE STOOD CONDEMNED

In the New Testament Jesus summarized God's rules in two seemingly simple commands. He said, "You shall love the Lord your God with all your heart and with all your soul and with all your mind. And . . . you shall love your neighbor as yourself" (Matt. 22:37–39). Since God declares that he hates injustice and that it's an abomination to him when a guilty person goes unpunished, our only hope of avoiding his just sentence is to obey these two rules. The problem we're all facing, though, if we're being honest, is that although these two commands seem easy, they're not easy to obey. It shouldn't be all that hard to love others, should it? And God is so good that love for him should be an automatic response.

The difficulty, of course, is that these rules involve our inner person: our mind, will, and emotions. If the command were simply, "Make up your bed when you get up," we might be able to do it. We could gut it out when we are happy, sad, angry, confused, or frustrated. And because that kind of command doesn't engage our hearts, we could even do it when we feel nothing but disdain for God. But his rules are more demanding than mere perfunctory duty. God's law demands an all-encompassing, white-hot love for him that is demonstrated in grateful holy living and joyful service of our neighbor. As Jesus said, it's a love that's so strong every other love looks like hatred in comparison to it (Luke 14:26). Love for God is the only motive that will suffice because "love is the fulfilling of the law" (Rom. 13:10). As commentator Matthew Henry wrote, "All obedience begins in the affections, and nothing in religion is done right, that is not done there first."[1]

Have you ever thought about how similar we all are to the rich young ruler who came to Jesus looking for commendation? Assured of his right standing before God, he boasted that he had kept all of God's commands from his youth. Don't murder—*check*. Don't commit adultery—*got it*. Don't lie, don't steal, honor your parents—*check, check, check*. But then Jesus touched him where he stood guilty before the bar of the Judge of heaven who looks on the heart. The young man thought this Prophet would be impressed with his goodness. Instead he discovered that all of his good works had been done while awaiting execution on death row. He didn't love God or his neighbor.

> "One thing you still lack. Sell all that you have and distribute to the poor, and you will have treasure in heaven; and come, follow me." But when he heard these things, he became very sad, for he was extremely rich. (Luke 18:22–23)

Wow! Stop for a moment and put yourself in this young man's place. How would you respond to that world-shattering command? Would you have gone away sad like he did? Oh, his response might have been, "I thought all you wanted was my outward behavior, not my heart! You want me to love you more than I love my wealth, status, privilege? You want me to love you more than I love my good reputation? I can't do that!" This wealthy young man learned that "God . . . is to be loved in the first place, and nothing loved beside him, but what is loved for him."[2] And with that understanding came realization of guilt and the just sentence of condemnation that hung over him. No wonder he went away intensely grieved.

Not only are we commanded to love God preeminently, but we're also to love our neighbor the way we love ourselves. What does our self-love look like? We love ourselves by always giving ourselves the benefit of the doubt, believing the best about our motives and actions, and striving to obtain for ourselves whatever we want.

Here are some questions for you to consider as you think about whether you love your neighbor: Out of love for your neighbor, have you always shared the good news of the gospel? Do you purposely take the middle seat on an airplane so that someone else won't have to? Have you always refrained from wishing that someone else's spouse/children/parent/job/gifting was yours instead of theirs? Do you keep yourself from jockeying for position at work or bragging about your accomplishments? Have you ever spoken to anyone, including your spouse, children, or parents, in an unkind or demeaning manner? Have you ever wished that a slow driver ahead of you would disappear? Do you show partiality to those who have the power to do you good and slight those who are less important?

Since John writes that it is impossible to love God and act in hateful ways to our neighbor (1 John 4:20), when we fail to love others, we're disobeying both of Jesus' commands at the same time. And just in case we think we haven't really been all that bad, James tells us that if we've broken just one part of the law only once, we're accountable for it all (James 2:10).

It's true: we don't love God and we don't love our neighbor—at least not as he has called us to. We've all broken a holy God's holy law, and if we're being honest we all know what we deserve. The verdict: guilty. The sentence: death. In God's eyes we're all David Westerfields, and if our God were like us, he wouldn't want us hanging around in his neighborhood either.

He Was Innocent

On the other hand, here's the record of your Savior, Jesus Christ. Look at all the ways he willingly obeyed the laws he decreed. Please notice that his obedience wasn't mere outward conformity. It was a demonstration of his holy passion to please his Father. He didn't obey because he had to; no, he wanted to obey because he loved his Father.

He said, "I always do the things that are pleasing to him" (John 8:29); "I do as the Father has commanded me, so that the world may know that I love the Father" (John 14:31); "My food is to do the will of him who sent me and to accomplish his work" (John 4:34); "I seek not my own will but the will of him who sent me" (John 5:30); "I do not [seek to] receive glory from people" (John 5:41); "I have come down . . . not to do my own will but the will of him who sent me" (John 6:38); "I have kept my Father's commandments" (John 15:10); "I . . . accomplished the work that [he] gave me to do" (John 17:4); "For their sake I consecrate myself, that they also may be sanctified" (John 17:19); "Love one another: just as I have loved you" (John 13:34); "[I] fulfill all righteousness" (Matt. 3:15).

Jesus is the one who has the authority to tell us to love the Father and our neighbor, because that was his lifelong testimony. If we're going to be true to our love of justice, the verdict that we should pronounce over him is "innocent." Not only was he not a guilty lawbreaker, but his active obedience was always driven by pure motives: love for the Father and those the Father had given him. He didn't love so that others would think highly of him or make his life trouble-free. No, he was holy because he loved holiness and his holy Father. What is the just sentence that we should pronounce on him, the faultless one? "Freedom! Blessing! Life!"

HE WAS CONDEMNED IN YOUR PLACE

But what was the "unjust" sentence he received instead? Death. Not just any death, either. He submitted to the ignominious death of crucifixion on a Roman cross. I'm afraid we've grown accustomed to that imagery. We wear gold crosses on our ears and paste cool Celtic crosses on our cars. Why, even Madonna wears a cross these days.

Would his death make more of an impact on you if I said that the innocent Lamb of God was electrocuted like some child-raping, mother-murdering, blaspheming, slave-trader—for our lack of love? Would it shock you if I said that he was strapped to a gurney, wheeled into a room before a self-righteous audience who despised him and gleefully cheered when he received a lethal injection—for our disobedience? Can you picture him before a firing squad, naked, blindfolded, with all the world looking on, confirmed in their belief that he was getting what he deserved, and executed like some perverted, hateful David Westerfield in our place? And as if all that weren't enough, the Father, his Father, around whom his entire existence orbited, poured out his wrath upon him and deserted him at the very moment of his death because, in all fairness, you have earned both wrath and desertion? This was the sentence carried out against the Sinless One.

THE GREAT EXCHANGE

How could the God who said that it was an "abomination" to punish the innocent or free the guilty predestine[3] this seemingly monstrous miscarriage of justice? He could righteously do so only by placing on the willing, Innocent One *all* of our sin and then condemning him for it. It's vital for us to reflect on both our disobedience and his punishment, if we're ever to fully live in the freedom he paid so dearly to secure for us. We've got to understand that he took all of our sin upon himself and then bore in his own person all of the punishment the Father justly demanded. He took it all—the sin we committed in our youth, the sin we committed before our conversion, the sin we committed today, and the sin we'll commit tomorrow. He didn't just bear the punishment for the time when we were trying to be good but flubbed up a little. He bore God's wrath for every time when we knew we shouldn't speak the way we were about to speak, but did it anyway. He received the righteous sentence for every unkind, lustful, selfish, wrathful, covetous, apathetic, vain, proud, dishonest, perverse thought, word, and deed that has ever proceeded from our hearts. The Father poured out *all* his wrath on his Son. There is no more left for you or me. He won't condemn you now because condemning the innocent is an abomination to him, and that's what he says you are: *innocent*. He won't punish you for your sins because to do so would be unjust; someone's already paid for those sins, and it would be unfair to punish you for them again.

Many people struggle with feelings of condemnation and guilt today because they've never really understood what Jesus did for them on Calvary. They think that their relationship with God is predicated on the fact that they're not really all that bad, and then they wonder if God still loves them when they struggle with ongoing sin. They wonder if they were ever really his. They don't see the depth of the sin that Christ bore in their place and so they can't comprehend the righteous fury he withstood for them nor the riches of the grace they've been given. I'm encouraging you now to fully embrace your sinfulness for one simple reason: so that you can fully embrace this great exchange, our "justification."

This is one of the primary places where understanding your new identity is crucial. When Paul wrote that there is now no longer any condemnation for you because you are "in" Christ, this is what he meant: when our Savior suffered on that tree, you were there, suffering, too; when he died under the immense wrath of God, you were with him. And when he rose victorious from the grave after having paid the full penalty for your sin, you rose also, and now you've ascended to the heavens where you're seated with him. Like the faithful Good Shepherd that he is, he has sought you out and bore you on his back all the way to your heavenly home. In the eyes of your Savior, "It is *truly* finished" and you're seated with him in heaven now.

Are you beginning to see how it's impossible for you to ever be condemned because you've already paid for your sins? You have a new identity, a righteous record; you have been declared innocent. Nothing can ever change that. Here's the testimony of some of the writers of the New Testament with some personal pronouns I've inserted:

• "Therefore, if [you are] in Christ, [you are] a new creation. The old has passed away; behold, the new has come. All this is from God, who through Christ reconciled [you] to himself . . . in Christ God was reconciling [you] to himself, not counting [your] trespasses against [you]. . . . For [your] sake he made him to be sin who knew no sin, so that in him [you] might become the righteousness of God" (2 Cor. 5:17–19, 21). You're completely and permanently new; you've got the righteousness of God!

- "For God has done what the law . . . could not do. By sending his own Son . . . he condemned sin in the flesh, in order that the righteous requirement of the law might be fulfilled in [you]" (Rom. 8:3–4). Because you're in Christ, you have fulfilled every requirement of the law!

- "Christ . . . suffered once for sins, the righteous for the unrighteous, that he might bring [you] to God" (1 Pet. 3:18). Christ Jesus suffered the death and punishment you should have suffered for one reason: that you might be in affectionate, intimate fellowship with him for all eternity.

Once, in a counseling session, someone answered a question I posed about Scripture in this way: "The verse that means the most to me," my friend said, "is the one where God declares that he was sorry he ever made man" (Gen. 6:6). I know that this might sound unusual, but as I've counseled people over the years and listened to their questions at conferences, I've been astounded at the number of times this kind of idea has come up. It's as though these people, Christians all, think that God felt some sort of obligation to save them but that he really doesn't like them very much. It's as though they think they're part of his family but suspect that if God could sit them in a corner with a dunce cap on, he'd happily do so. Dear sister or brother, nothing is farther from the truth! God loves you so much that he sent his Son to suffer for sin, the righteous for the unrighteous, so that he might bring you to himself! Is this the action of someone who isn't filled with fervent love for you?

You Stand Justified[4]

Here's the reality of the great exchange: our sinful record became his, and he suffered the punishment we deserved. But that's not all he has done. If it were, that would be a great blessing, indeed. To stand innocent—to be back where our first parents were in the garden—would certainly be wondrous. But he hasn't left us there where Adam began. No, through the Second Adam, he has done even more for us; he has justified us. As you probably know, this concept of the great exchange is often referred to as justification. I've heard the word *justified* defined as "just as if I'd never sinned." And while that's true as far as it goes, it doesn't go far enough. Not only do we have a clean slate as Adam did, we've got something written on that slate that is so amazing I can scarcely believe it: Jesus' perfect record has become ours. Because God has accredited or imputed Jesus' perfect obedience to you, when God looks upon you, he sees you as a person who

- always does the things that are pleasing to him;
- is so focused on accomplishing his will and work that doing so is your daily food;
- doesn't seek your own will but seeks his will instead;
- doesn't seek to receive glory (praise, respect, worship) from others;
- has always kept all his commandments;
- lives in such a way that your life brings holiness to others;
- loves others and lays down your life on a consistent basis;
- lives in such a way that the people around you know that you love your heavenly Father more than anything else;
- seeks to obey every command so that righteousness will be fulfilled.

In God's opinion (the only one that matters!) that's your record today. One time during a conversation with a friend about these truths, she asked, "Isn't God just kidding himself?" I was glad to hear that question because it let me know that she was dealing with the full implications of grace and justification. These truths ought to astound us.

GOD'S LOVE FOR HIS SON

I'll admit that sometimes I cast about for assurance when I feel the creeping doubt and despair that infect my heart as I struggle with sin. When I look through all the closets of my soul and all I find is lovelessness, I know that I don't have any claim to God's love on my own. The only truth that can assuage is this: *I know that God loves his Son.* Even though there are times when I wonder how God can love me, I know that he loves his Son, and because he has made a formal, legal declaration that I'm *in* him, then I must continue to tell myself and believe that he loves me because of him. My only other option is to say that he doesn't love his Son at all. But the truth is that the pronouncement he made over him, "This is my beloved Son, with whom I am well pleased" (Matt. 3:17), he has now made over us: "This is my beloved daughter, this is my beloved son, all in whom I am well pleased." Will God ever push us away or keep us at arm's length? Would he push his Son away? Will God ever fail to hear our prayer? Does he hear his Son's? Is he disgusted with us and disappointed that he ever adopted us? Does Jesus disgust and disappoint him?

The Specters of Condemnation

Because there are times when our feelings of guilt or condemnation flow out of a superficial understanding of our sinfulness, I've belabored the point about our failures in this chapter. Although it seems counterintuitive, fully embracing our utter inability to keep the law will actually free us from feelings of guiltiness. For instance, when your children fail and you respond to them in an ungodly way it's easy to beat yourself up with thoughts such as "I'm such a terrible mother." If, however, you've been freed from the expectation that you should be able to be a wonderful mother, your heart's response will be:

> I know that I've failed to be the kind of mother he wants me to be, but that's why I need a Savior, and it's why my kids need one, too. Thank you, Lord, that you've given me your perfect record, and that even though I sin, I am accounted perfectly righteous before you. Please forgive me and help me respond to this great gift you've given in faith and grateful obedience. I trust you to work in me.

In my own life I frequently have to pray in this way numbers of times before I can silence the dreadful harping of my proud heart. I have to remind myself over and over that his righteousness is now mine and that the way my heart harasses me is more a function of my pride and self-sufficiency than a sincere desire for godliness. If godliness before him is what I was really after, then one look at the cross and empty tomb would suffice. But I can see that I'm frequently more concerned about whether I approve of myself than the fact that he approves of me. I sinfully long to be able to look at my life and feel good about my personal accomplishments—*See what a good mother I am!*—and it's that desire that spawns crushing guilt. The only way to silence my heart and find solace is to continually remind myself of my new identity in Christ and to be satisfied with that alone. If I try to be satisfied in my own accomplishments or identity, I'll never know the comfort he promised. "Come to me, all who labor and are heavy laden," he calls, "and I will give you rest. Take my yoke upon you, and learn from me, for I am gentle and lowly in heart, and you will find rest for your souls. For my yoke is easy, and my burden is light" (Matt. 11:28–30).

When I come to him in meekness and dependence, I'll learn the difference between proud self-condemnation (which is all about me) and humble conviction of sin (which is about him, his grace, and his law). His yoke is easy; his burden is light. I can come to him and find rest for my soul, but I must come in humility and brokenness (1 Pet. 5:5).

In addition, I know there are times when feelings of condemnation plague us because we think that God's love is like ours. Instead of basking in the goodness of his grace, we wonder if he'll reject us because we're quick to reject others. It's at times like this that we have to remember that God isn't like us. He doesn't love us because we're lovable; no, his love is predicated solely upon his gracious choice. Remember, his love came to us when we were his enemies. Why would he leave us now that we're his beloved children? When your heart accuses you and says, "You're so worthless. Look at the way you've failed him again!" you can confidently answer, "It is true that on my own I am worthless, but he has made me completely righteous in his Son. He has declared that he loves me and his love is now the most important thing about me. I believe that he won't stop loving me until he stops loving his own Son. I can begin to serve him again because I know he is here, with me, sustaining me and granting me his grace."

David Westerfield No More

The thought that I want you to carry away from this chapter is that although you had the record of a David Westerfield before God, you have it no longer. I can remember many nights as a young, unsaved child when I prayed that I would do better, be a better person, only to discover the next day that I was the same old failure that I always had been. I'm thankful now, though, because God has answered those prayers through his Son. I'm not successful because I've finally gotten my act together. My heart has been quieted by his love because I recognize that he has regenerated, washed, forgiven, redeemed, and reconciled me. That old person I used to be is dead. A new person with an entirely new identity has arisen in her place: a woman about whom God has declared, "This is my beloved daughter—she brings me pleasure."

Can you say the same thing? If you're in Christ, that's God's precious thought of you. You bring him pleasure, because you have come to him and he has made you perfectly pleasing to himself.

As of this writing, David Westerfield is in prison, awaiting execution. How would he react if the warden came to him and said, "The court has found someone else guilty of your crime and he will be punished in your place. You are free to go and the record of your conviction has been completely expunged. You've been given a perfectly just record in place of the one you earned. No one will remember this about you any more. You're completely free." How would he respond? How will you?

REALIZING HOW GOD'S LOVE TRANSFORMS YOUR IDENTITY AND LIFE

1) "He who justifies the wicked and he who condemns the righteous are both alike an abomination to the LORD" (Prov. 17:15). Explain how God can justify the "wicked" and condemn the "righteous" without being unjust.

2) What does it mean to be justified? How does your justification affect your daily life? How does it affect your struggle with self-condemnation?

3) "The acceptance of the believer with God is perfect the moment he believes because Christ and his work are perfect. The status of the believer can never be improved upon—he possesses all the riches of Christ."[5] How would your life be different if you consistently acted on this truth: you possess all the perfection and riches of Christ and nothing can ever change that?

4) Summarize in four or five sentences what you learned from this chapter.

CHAPTER FIVE

YOUR INHERITANCE

Now we have received . . . the Spirit who is from God, that we might understand the things freely given us by God.

1 CORINTHIANS 2:12

At one point in the classic allegory *Pilgrim's Progress*, Christian and Hopeful found themselves imprisoned in Doubting Castle, dominated by the spiteful giant, Despair. After spending several days in cruel suffering beneath his malicious rule, the friends grew despondent and started to believe the lies Despair was telling them. They questioned whether they would ever be free again. In addition to this torment of soul, they were in great physical pain from the wounds that their malevolent captor inflicted upon them. They reeled from the effects of his hateful advice: "You are in a hopeless situation. The only way you'll ever be free of this wretchedness and misery is to end your life. Don't expect anyone to help you! You've brought this misery upon yourself by failing to stay on the right path. You deserve every ounce of the punishment I'm giving you and you'll never be free again!"

Day by day he asserted that they would never escape his dungeon and that he would ultimately destroy them, as he had other wayward travelers. They would languish in this dank prison until they finally succumbed to a terrifying death. Sick at heart and utterly hopeless, poor Christian began to contemplate suicide.

"Brother," pleaded Christian, "what shall we do? The life that we now live is miserable. For my part I know not whether it is best, to live thus, or to die out of hand. . . . Shall we be ruled by the giant?"[1]

Then, when most despondent, when Christian had decided to take his own life, he was reminded of God's gift to him: "What a fool," quoth he, "am I thus to lie in this stinking dungeon, while I may as well walk at liberty! I have a key in my bosom called Promise, that will, I am persuaded, open any lock in Doubting Castle."[2]

Soon, both Christian and Hopeful were free of Doubting Castle and back on the path to the Celestial City.

Understanding Your Promised Inheritance

Just as Christian and Hopeful needed to be reminded of God's promises in order to escape the vile grasp of Despair, so we, too, need to understand the fullness of the inheritance we've been given in the gospel. You see, we're not "in" Christ in some non-familial, detached way. Instead, we're actually Christ's brothers (John 20:17; Rom. 8:29), members of his household, and therefore heirs and recipients with him of *all* his Father's riches (Gal. 4:7).

This endowment is so extraordinary (and so wonderful!); we cannot comprehend it without the enabling help of the Spirit. Because of this, God has graciously sent him to us so that we "might understand the things freely given" to us by God (1 Cor. 2:12). Instead of thinking that God wants to keep his treasure hidden from us until we're worthy to receive it, we need to believe that he is intensely interested in our knowing what our inheritance is *now* while we're in such need. He wants us to make full use of his Keys of Promise so that we might drive out all the lies of Giant Despair.

Embracing Your Inheritance

As my mom has had some unusual health concerns of late, we've been discussing her assets and what her will would be for my brother and me if something should happen to her. We have a very open relationship about these matters, and being the woman of faith that she is, she's comfortable talking about how she wants her assets divided.

In contrast, I do recognize that in many families talking about one's inheritance is looked down on as the lowest form of money-grubbing. But God's perspective on your inheritance is anything but typical. In fact, your Father's generous desire is that you fight for your inheritance with all your strength because this brings him glory.

God is glorified when you appropriate your inheritance, because it shows the world how great his love, mercy, and generosity are. It shows his greatness in that just as it takes a death to execute a will, so it took a death to open your inheritance to you. It took the death of the Son. He wants you to appreciate that death and savor all that it brings to you.

Think for a moment how disappointing it would be to my mother if she had worked diligently to provide an extensive inheritance for me, but I told her I was going to leave the money in the bank and never use it. She would be particularly disheartened if she discovered that I would rather live on the street as a homeless person, begging for my next meal, than use what she'd provided for me. It wouldn't be an act of love and humility for me to refuse her gift; no, it would be hatred. The joy that she would have experienced in providing for me would be significantly diminished if she saw that I was too self-reliant, unbelieving, or proud to receive it from her.

One part of your Father's joy in giving you an inheritance is watching you discover and utilize it. Rather than trying to prove our innate strength to him, he is most glorified when our weakness teaches us to pursue all he has provided for us. He is glorified and blessed when our life reflects the riches of his grace—riches that he has "lavished" upon us! (Eph. 1:6, 8). Too often, we're like poor Christian, living in doubt and despair, when we've got sure promises given to us that would free and cheer us. Our faithful intercessor, Jesus Christ, has sent the Spirit so that we'll know and enjoy all he has bequeathed to us.

Because we're going to look at a small part of our wonderful inheritance now, let me encourage you to take a few moments to ask the Spirit to help you "understand the things freely given" to you by God. These gospel truths are foolishness to the natural man, but to us who've been given the mind of Christ, they are magnificent. "'What no eye has seen, nor ear heard, nor the heart of man imagined, what God has prepared for those who love him'—these things God has revealed *to us* through the Spirit" (1 Cor. 2:9–10). What has God prepared for you?

Understanding Your Inheritance

Everlasting Happiness in Him

The quintessence of this inheritance is our relationship with and access to the Lord God. Just as the Levites received no share in the land because they had been granted a gift greater than mere property,[3] so our souls have been granted a treasure better than anything we might attain in our own strength. He has granted us the true soul satisfaction of fellowship with the One for whom we were created. Because he has graciously granted to us both the capacity and desire to know him, we can be truly contented in him alone. He is the Fountainhead from which all the joy we desire incessantly streams. By his grace, we are emboldened to approach him with the most personal terms, "Abba, Father," and to know that he enjoys seeing us, runs to us, embraces and kisses us, as he welcomes us to himself (Luke 15:20)! Augustine simply stated, "God is man's happiness." He has granted us that happiness in himself, for in his "presence there is fullness of joy; at [his] right hand are pleasures forevermore" (Ps. 16:11). Are you aware of his presence now? Do you know that you're seated with Christ at his right hand just as surely as you're reading this page?

Have you ever wondered what makes the good news (or gospel), good news? Is it primarily good because through it you receive a "Get Out of Jail Free" card? No. It is the "good news of happiness"[4] because through it you are bound once and for all time to the

One who inclined your heart to desire happiness in the first place. He made you desire him, and he has answered your desire.

Why are the people "whose God is the LORD" happy? (Ps. 144:15 NKJV)? They are happy because they have access to his presence. *This* is what makes the good news good. This is the highest and best inheritance you have, for as John Piper writes:

> All the saving events and all the saving blessing of the gospel are means of getting obstacles out of the way so that we might know and enjoy God most fully. Propitiation, redemption, forgiveness, imputation, sanctification, liberation, healing, heaven—none of these is good news except for one reason: they bring us to God for our everlasting enjoyment of him.[5]

Eternal Life in His Presence

Our relationship with God not only brings us the unceasing delight of his nearness, but it also brings us eternal life. This life begins the moment we're born again and is inextinguishable. Our Lord wants to assure us about eternal life so that we might know, and never again doubt, that it is ours. In the plainest of terms he said that if we believe in him we *will not perish* but will have eternal life (John 3:16), a gift he is qualified to bestow (John 10:28). We have inherited eternal life simply through belief in the Son, and this blessing is ours now and forever.

If you've been a Christian for any length of time, I know that the inheritance of eternal life might seem a little unexciting to you. *Eternal life, yes, I know, isn't that nice?* Perhaps it would be helpful if I put the promise of eternal life into perspective. The prospect of eternal life is in contrast to eternal "weeping and gnashing of teeth."[6] Because our souls are immortal, the opposite of eternal life isn't eternal death; it isn't a cessation of sentience. The Bible speaks terrifyingly of the prospect of ceaseless dying while we yet live on, where there will never be any hope of an end to the suffering, eternal dying without the welcome relief of death.

The lack of eternal life might be compared in some faint way to Christian's experience in Doubting Castle being bludgeoned day after day by the hateful club of Giant Despair. It would truly be hell to remember (and never forget!) that you once held the Key of Promise in your hand but had forever discarded it in self-reliance and unbelief. To be cut off from God's blessing of mercy, to know that you've made a mistake from which you will never recover, to never have another chance—these are the thoughts that will eternally terrify the soul who hasn't inherited eternal life.

All people, believers and unbelievers alike, live now in the light of God's common grace. There isn't a place on earth where his blessing isn't experienced in some sense.[7] But there is a place where those without eternal life will fully understand the anguish in Christ's cry, "My God, why have you forsaken me?" The opposite of the eternal life you've inherited is the anguish of being forsaken by God *forever* (1 Thess. 1:9).

I have written about eternal suffering because I want you to savor and employ the full blessing of your inheritance. Rather than relegating eternal life to a future day, we must realize that we possess his life now, especially on those days when we struggle against unbelief and sin and are tempted to think that he is so disappointed in us that he has to forsake us. The gospel tells us that being forsaken is part of the punishment for sin that our Savior bore in our place. If you are in Christ, no matter what your day has been like, no matter how many ways you blew it, his life is yours. "His mercies are new every morning" because he is faithful to renew and sustain those who are his (Lam. 3:22–24); indeed *mercy* is what he has declared over you. His love has forever banished the futility and regret of eternal condemnation from your soul. Unwavering faithfulness is his distinctive, not ours.

In some ways, though, we're still awaiting the full realization of the benefits of eternal life. Because we haven't yet experienced it in full, we're still anticipating the dawning of the day when separation and failure will vanish like the morning mist. In the meantime, though, we must continue to preach this truth to our hearts: a day will come when because he is so near to us, all our doubt, unbelief, and sin will be burned away by the light of his presence. With that day in view, we can persevere in our struggle on this day.

Reconciliation and Peace with Him

"Therefore, since we have been justified by faith, we have peace with God through our Lord Jesus Christ" (Rom. 5:1). How long has it been since the wonder of these words struck your heart? We've been granted complete reconciliation and peace with the Holy King of Heaven. We don't have to go around thinking that he is angry with us or hostile to us. No, he is at peace with us.

Please don't be confused here. The peace that God has granted us is indeed a calmness of soul, but it is not primarily that. It is the cessation of hostility between us rebels and a righteous omnipotent ruler. In granting us peace, he is saying that although we were once his enemies, he has removed the opposition that he had toward us. We who were once children under his wrath (Eph. 2:3) have now been brought near through the blood of Christ (2:13). We who were once "alienated and hostile in mind . . . he has now reconciled in his body of flesh by his death" (Col. 1:21–22). *The payment he demanded, he has provided.* He is not like some pagan god, demanding a blood sacrifice to appease his capricious wrath. No, he is a holy King who's been deeply offended by our rebellion but has taken the punishment he demanded for that sin and placed it entirely upon himself. Because of this, we no longer need to fear approaching him with our sin. *All* the just wrath he felt toward his rebellious children was spent on his Son. We can come boldly before him now, without trembling and in confidence. When we approach him, he extends his scepter of peace toward us and speaks words of welcome.

Why are reconciliation and peace so very significant? They are significant because many serious-minded believers go through their day under a dreadful cloud of gloom. They read that their God is a God of love, but that truth doesn't impact their hearts. They live in fear that he'll notice them, as though they were in Mordor with Sauron's all-seeing eye relentlessly searching for a reason to punish them. Although nothing could be further from the truth, this kind of fear-driven existence makes sense if we're trying to live a godly life while ignoring the gospel. Only the gospel can calm our hearts and make us able to stand courageously before him. Only the wrath-bearing Christ can give us the assurance we need to stand transparent before the One whose eyes search out everything, even the hidden person of the heart. Right on the heels of the seemingly terrifying statement, "No creature is hidden from his sight, but all are naked and exposed to the eyes of him to whom we must give account," comes the reassuring message:

> Since then we have a great high priest who has passed through the heavens, Jesus, the Son of God, let us hold fast our confession. For we do not have a high priest who is unable to sympathize with our weaknesses, but one who in every respect has been tempted as we are, yet without sin. Let us then with confidence draw near to the throne of grace, that we may receive mercy and find grace to help in time of need. (Heb. 4:13–16)

We can hold fast because he has passed through the heavens and is interceding for us, providing mercy, grace, and help in our great need. He is no longer our enemy; he's not angry. He has made peace with us at great cost to himself.

When we struggle with sin and wonder if our faith pleases him, or if he is, in fact, with us, we can know with certainty that he is now and always will be completely reconciled to us. Would he ever tell the Son that his sacrifice just wasn't sufficient and he has more wrath to pour out? Of course not. And he won't say that to us either.

We've Been Redeemed

In our sedentary society, we're encouraged to pursue regular exercise. My personal preference is swimming, while others enjoy biking, elliptical machines, or treadmills. In Victorian England, however, treadmills weren't found in air-conditioned health clubs—they were found in prisons.

Treadmills, or treadwheels, as they were called, were used in penal servitude as a form of punishment. Some treadwheels were productive, grinding wheat or transporting water, but others were purely punitive in nature. Prisoners were punished by spending the bulk of their day walking up an inclined plane, knowing that all their hard labor was for nothing. The only hope the prisoner had was that, at some day in the future, he would have "paid his debt" to society and would be set free. He couldn't even look on his labor at the end of the day and know that, if nothing else, he'd been productive.

Before our loving Father redeemed us, we were prisoners to sin (John 8:34). Whether we were fully aware of it or not, we spent our life in futility, walking uphill, going nowhere, producing nothing of value, awaiting eternal punishment. It didn't matter how nicely we decorated our treadmill or how hard we tried to excel at walking; we weren't lessening our debt in any way by all our effort. In fact, we were increasing it.

Part of your inheritance is that although you once were enslaved to sin, Christ paid the ransom that purchased your freedom. He promised, "If the Son sets you free, you will be free indeed" (John 8:36). By paying the price you were unable to pay, he has set you free from slavery to sin, and you've become not merely a slave or servant of another, but a son of God! The debt you owed a holy God for violating his righteous law hasn't been merely ignored; it has been paid in full. Christ's blood is the "ransom" by which we've been delivered from slavery to sin and every consequence of that bondage. So, as Puritan William Cowper penned, "He is the free-man whom the truth makes free, and all are slaves beside."[8] You're no longer a slave to sin! You're now a son!

The Love of Christ for Orphans

As of September 2005, there were approximately 500,000 children in foster care in the United States.[9] The majority of these poor children were born to parents who didn't want them or were unable to care for them and so were shuffled off to live with other families for a variety of reasons. Wondering who you are, wondering if you would ever be loved or where you belong, would be a very sad way to spend a childhood.

Though the foster care situation is troubling, there's a reality even more tragic: many of us live as though we were spiritual foster children. Although we give tacit assent to our adoption into God's family, we struggle to believe that his commitment to be our Father isn't dependent *in any way* on our daily performance.

You can judge whether you're functioning as a foster child by how you respond to both sin and suffering. When you sin, are you drawn *first* to the cross or to an examination of your record? Does your sin make you thankful for Jesus? Does it make you love him more, or do you want to push him away? Are you quick to repent, or do you hide out, hoping to make it up and do better next time? Have you ever said anything like "I know I really blew it that time, but I'll do better if you give me another chance"? If so, you're still living like a foster child.

Secondly, when you face trial or suffering, is your first response to look back over your life to see if there is some reason God should be punishing you? Do you scrutinize the performance of your daily disciplines? *How's my prayer life? Did I read my Bible? Maybe I should have fasted yesterday.* Do you rake over every thought, word, and deed searching for some failure that makes you deserving of this trouble? Have you ever asked, what did I do to deserve this? Or, are you tempted to think that God capriciously doles out blows like some drunken abuser or is just biding his time till he can get rid of you?

Although God does discipline or train us as the Master Teacher he is (Heb. 12:5ff.), his work in our lives is *never* punitive; it is *always* redemptive. This means that he doesn't punish us for our sin, but rather that, because of his great love, he gently and lovingly frees us from the lies, misconceptions, and idolatries that captivate and enslave our hearts. He *never* punishes us in wrath because he has no wrath left. Every drop of his wrath was *all* poured out on his Son.

Only foster children (or the children of abusers) believe that their position in the family is so tenuous that their day-to-day failures might eventuate in cruelty or abandonment. If you view the trials in your life as punishments from the hands of a wrathful God, the gospel has lost its impact on your soul. You've forgotten that you've been adopted by the holy, loving, and pure Father who has pledged himself to you and sealed that pledge in blood.

It's essential that we cease living like foster children, because living in slavish fear of punishment or abandonment will breed over-scrupulous introspection and works righteousness. Walking on eggshells, being on our best behavior, making up for yesterday's failures, won't foster true godliness. No, it will only result in further lawlessness and self-condemnation, because living under law (any law!) will always and only create more sin (see Romans 7). *Christian obedience has to be motivated by love for God in response to his great grace, or it is destined to fail.* And it can only be motivated by love when we know that our relationship with our heavenly Father is eternally secure.

If we want to know the fullness of God's grace, life, and power in our daily lives, there's only one way to do so. We've got "to know the love of Christ that surpasses knowledge" (Eph. 3:19). Remembering Christ's love in the gospel is not merely the invitation into God's family, but it is also the foundation of our experience of his person. Only constant meditation on Christ's love will make us eager to be with him. Without it, we'll be too afraid to be that close to him and, although we'll seek to serve him, we won't ever really let him in.

He Is Guarding Our Inheritance

Blessed be the God and Father of our Lord Jesus Christ! According to his great mercy, he has caused us to be born again to a living hope through the resurrection of Jesus Christ from the dead, *to an inheritance that is imperishable, undefiled, and unfading, kept in heaven for you, who by God's power are being guarded through faith* for a salvation ready to be revealed in the last time. (1 Pet. 1:3–5)

How did we inherit all these riches? Through the death and resurrection of the Son who brought us new birth. We've been begotten by him! But even though this is true, how do we know these riches will last? We know because they're being *guarded in heaven by God* for us. Think of it: our inheritance is being kept for us while we're being kept by him.

We've inherited great riches, haven't we? We've got new life now that will fit us for heaven, but not even that is the greatest joy we've been given. The greatest joy of all is to have God to be all our own. God himself has declared, "I will be their God, and they shall be my people" (Jer. 31:33).

REMEMBERING YOUR KEY OF PROMISE

As I struggle with what seems like endless sin in my life, it's easy for me to become discouraged and wonder if I'll ever change. Why did I snap at her like that again? Why is it so hard for me to be genuinely kind to him? When will I ever overcome this selfishness? These are questions that plague my heart as the war against my sin seems interminable. Then, if I'm not careful, my thoughts quickly morph into despair, and I doubt that the inheritance is mine at all. Thoughts of faithless resignation creep into the dark recesses of my mind, and I descend into an abyss of unbelief and hopelessness. It's at times like this that the Spirit faithfully reminds me, like Christian, the way out of Doubting Castle is found in the Key of Promise. "Spirit, help me," I cry. "Remind me of my inheritance! Give me faith to believe your promises and continue on in this battle! Silence the giant Despair, help me out of this dungeon and grant me strength to pick up the sword again!"

All of us are, at some point, in need of being reminded of the riches of our inheritance. Perhaps what you need to call to mind is that God has promised himself to you. This is the best news you could ever hear. You are welcome in his presence, he's yours! Even though you may have been deserted by a loved one or betrayed by a friend, your near kinsman is the fountain of all joys and he has promised that he'll never, ever, no never forsake you (Heb. 13:5).

Perhaps you're suffering from a lingering physical pain or an endless fear of the future and you need to remember that you've got eternal life now. Employ his promise that the days of weeping and "gnashing of teeth" for you will indeed end. Your enemy and your faithless heart are lying when they tell you that your circumstances will never change. An endless day of joy is coming and *nothing can avert its dawning*. You could as easily stop the revolution of the earth around the sun as you could stop the dawning of that day!

If you lack assurance, feel plagued by your failures or wrongly believe that God is in a perpetual state of being ticked off at you, remember that his Son bore every drop of wrath against you and that he is completely and irrevocably reconciled to you. There's no more wrath to be had. His disposition toward you today is what it has been since he made you his own: he loves you and longs for you to know it and savor every drop of it.

As you struggle with your ongoing sin and idolatry, remember that he has set you free *indeed* and that you're no longer sentenced to be chained to the treadmill of sin and failure. He has paid the ransom demanded for your release from sin, and you're now walking in the freedom of the glory of the sons and daughters of God. You've been given the ability to say no to sin and yes to righteousness. You're freed from the law and from slavery to sin—free to live out your life in humble repentance and grateful obedience.

In the next chapter we'll look at the only qualification you need to receive this glorious inheritance: faith. In the meantime, though, let me encourage you to review the Keys of Promise you've been given and ask the Spirit to help you employ them today—they're all yours for the taking.

Realizing How God's Love Transforms Your Identity and Life

1) Martin Luther wrote, "The inheritance is simply eternal salvation."[10] What are the facets of your inheritance that mean the most to you? Why?

2) A. W. Tozer wrote, "The man who has God for his treasure has all things in one. Many ordinary treasures may be denied him, or if he is allowed to have them, the enjoyment of them will be so tempered that they will never be necessary to his happiness. Or if he must see them go, one after one, he will scarcely feel a sense of loss, for having the Source of all things he has in One all satisfaction, all pleasure, all delight."[11] Respond to his thoughts.

3) Do you live like a foster child? How do you respond to your own sin? Are you comforted by Christ's perfections and love, or do you try to hide from him until you can do better? How do you respond to suffering? Are you tempted to believe that God is punishing you? What is the difference between punishment and redemptive discipline?

4) In this short chapter we didn't consider the glorious fact that God calls us *his* inheritance! We're his "own possession" (1 Pet. 2:9), his treasure. We're called to him so that we might live to "the praise of his glory" (Eph. 1:12; see also Isa. 62:3, Zech. 9:16). What is the inheritance that he has in you? Why would he call you his treasure?

5) Summarize in four or five sentences what you've learned from this chapter.

LOOK AND LIVE!

*And as Moses lifted up the serpent in the wilderness, so must the Son
of Man be lifted up, that whoever believes in him may have eternal
life.*

JOHN 3:14—15

U nder the cover of darkness, while the rest of Jerusalem was
in preparation for the Passover celebration, a religious leader
surreptitiously sought out an audience with a popular itinerant
preacher. He didn't know he was about to come face-to-face with
the eternal Lamb of God; he didn't realize that his life, as he had
come to know it, was about to end.

"'Rabbi,' he said, 'we all know that God has sent you to teach
us. Your miraculous signs are evidence that God is with you'" (John
3:1 NLT).

Not dissimilar to the rich young ruler, Nicodemus probably
anticipated a polite rejoinder in response to this respectful greeting.
But Jesus was never one to waste time by exchanging inane cour-
tesies. He had known Nicodemus's name since before the foundation of the world, so he immediately set about preparing him for
inclusion into his family. Oblivious to his blindness and the mortal
wound in his soul, there was only one way Nicodemus could gain
eternal life: his self-trust, self-righteousness, and self-rule would
have to be annihilated.

"Truly, truly, I say to you, unless one is born again he cannot see
the kingdom of God" (John 3:3).

"What's that you're saying?" an astonished Nicodemus stammered. "I don't understand. How could I do that? Surely you don't mean . . ."

"Truly, truly, I say to you," the pounding continued, "unless one is born of water and the Spirit, he cannot enter the kingdom of God" (John 3:5).

But how? Christ's words were so world-shattering, Nicodemus must have felt as though he had plunged headlong into an icy maelstrom of confusion where every cherished belief was torn from his grasp, where all sure ground had sunk beneath turbulent waters. "I know this man is from God because I've seen what he can do. He is not mad, but what's this he is saying? Have I gone mad? How can I be born again? How could I possibly . . . ?"

Overflowing with gracious mercy, Nicodemus's Savior continued on with the demolition of every vestige of this Pharisee's proud self-confidence.

This is something that can only be accomplished by the Spirit. "Are you the teacher of Israel and yet you do not understand these [simple] things?" (v. 10). The Fisher of Men expertly placed the hook within Nicodemus's soul. Pious, scholarly Nicodemus was helpless. He could no more bring about eternal life within his heart than he could accomplish his own conception in his mother's womb. He needed help from without—help from a startling quarter.

"As Moses lifted up the serpent in the wilderness, so must the Son of Man be lifted up, that whoever believes in him may have eternal life" (vv. 14–15).

Question upon question must have filled his mind: "What? The serpent in the wilderness? Am I part of that unbelieving, God-dishonoring rabble who died under Jehovah's wrath in the desert? Do you think I've been infected by some imperceptible venom? Is that who I am? Who are you? Are you the bronze serpent? How will you be 'lifted up'? What are you calling me to believe?"

Three years later the Spirit would remind Nicodemus of Christ's words. He would undoubtedly gaze upon the bloody Calvary scene, and he would believe and live. "Ah, now I understand. You are the bronze serpent and there you are, lifted up between heaven and earth for me to see." Though nailed to a cross, the Savior's hands opened his blind eyes, stopped the decay of a soul infected by death's sting, and turned him fully toward himself so Nicodemus could look on him and live.

Like Nicodemus, I'm sure you, too, are familiar with the Old Testament story of fiery snakes and a bronze serpent dangling from a pole. But since our Lord thought that understanding this story was key to understanding his mission and our response to it, let me remind you of it again.[1]

SERPENTS IN THE WILDERNESS

Because the Israelites had incessantly complained against the Lord, he sent fiery serpents to chasten them. Many of the Israelites were bitten and had died, and many others were soon to join them. "We've sinned," the people said. "We've dishonored God with our complaints. Pray for us and ask God to take his judgment away" (see Num. 21:4–9). I've tried to put myself in this story: How would I have reacted? What would I have thought or said?

As a grandmother, I shudder to think of the terror of watching my children or grandchildren being bitten by fiery serpents. I would have searched frantically for a cure. I would have held them tight and sought to comfort them. *Oh God, oh God, help us!* I would have hoped against hope that the overwhelming force of my love would be enough to cure them. *Please, Lord, oh please, help us!* Then as I watched them writhe in pain, I would have sent my husband to Moses. *Plead with him to pray for us! Tell him we're sorry for complaining. Ask him to take the sickness away! Run, please, run! Find a cure, bring deliverance!*

I can't imagine the confusion, anger, hopelessness, and fear that would have filled my heart when I heard of the Lord's strange remedy. "Moses is making a metal snake and he'll place it on a pole and Jehovah has promised that all who look at it will live." *What? How would that help? What we need is* real *help, a powerful antidote, someone to tell us how to fight this poison, not some weak symbol of a snake hanging on a pole!*

But perhaps one of my little ones would hear the strange words being reported and she would cry out, "Help me! Pick me up so I can see! I can't turn my head. Turn me toward that pole. I know that if I can just see it I will be cured." And then, in desperation, I would turn her little head and stand amazed as her muscles relaxed and a life-giving flow enveloped and healed her.

FAITH IN THE GOD WHO LOVES US

I'm sure that Nicodemus, being an intellectual leader, understood the historical facts surrounding the story we've just reviewed. Even so, he was utterly blind to its true significance. He didn't know that it revealed a God whose love was so powerful and whose mercy was so abundant, that he would send "his own Son in the likeness of sinful flesh" to be a "curse" for him (Rom. 8:3; Gal. 3:13). He didn't know he was conversing with the Bronze Serpent in living form. Nicodemus was utterly undone in one short conversation with the Christ. He was loved, and that love was powerful enough to both slay and resurrect him.

So far in this book I've called your attention to some of the wonderful blessings that are yours through the good news of the gospel. Because of God's love, we've got an entirely new identity; we've been adopted, reconciled, redeemed, forgiven, and justified. As wonderful as these gifts are, I'm sure you know that they aren't given universally to everyone. There is one qualification for the reception of these blessings; that qualification is faith.

Faith is another one of those well-worn concepts that we're vaguely familiar with but usually can't quite define. Most of us know that we're saved by faith alone, but what does that actually mean? What does saving faith consist of? Are there particular doctrines that I must assent to? Is faith more than mere assent? Where does it come from?

I find it very instructive that the first statement Jesus makes after the bronze serpent foreshadowing is a powerful declaration of God's love: "And as Moses lifted up the serpent in the wilderness, so must the Son of Man be lifted up, that whoever believes in him may have eternal life. For God so loved the world, that he gave his only Son, that whoever believes in him should not perish but have eternal life" (John 3:14–16).

"God so loved . . . that he sent" are his words. Faith begins, then, with an invitation to look to the One he sent. God initiates the transaction by lovingly sending, and he asks us to respond to his compassionate generosity by believing that he is *that* good. *You are mortally wounded, but I love you. Look to me. I have provided all the cure you need.* It continues with a promise: *If you believe in me I will give you eternal life.*

Faith, then, is simply a believing that there is a God who loves us, in spite of the poison of sin coursing through our soul. It is a believing that he loves us even though, like the Israelites of old, we have nothing to bring to him but malignancy, wretched sickness, and grumbling misery. It is believing that he invites us to look to him, to rely upon him, and to trust in him simply to do what he has said. It is believing that if we turn the gaze of our soul upward toward him, he will give us life. The Lord Jesus characterizes the simplicity and certainty of saving faith, stating that it is his Father's will to grant eternal life to all who *look on* and *believe in* him. "For this is the will of my Father, that everyone who *looks on* the Son and *believes in* him should have eternal life, and I will raise him up on the last day" (John 6:40).

SOUL-SAVING EYE EXERCISES

Stop reading for a moment. Look up from this page and fasten your eyes on something else and then come back to your reading. Do you see that in one very important sense, that's all that he has required of you? The shifting of your eyes from this page to another object doesn't require great skill, deep understanding, or monumental strength. It simply requires a desire to do so. That's what faith is—a looking away from yourself to Someone else.

While that is a true definition of faith, it needs to be somewhat expanded. To help you understand what true faith is, think again with me about that little child in the wilderness. If she had looked with mere scoffing at the bronze serpent or just glanced at it in curiosity, it wouldn't have been an agent of healing for her, would it? It didn't contain any magical powers in and of itself.[2] In the same way, I'm pretty sure there were people standing about at the foot of the cross, watching the Lord die, who did not automatically inherit eternal life. No, the bronze serpent and the crucified Son are agents of healing *only* when our gaze gives evidence to the simple belief that good will come to us from God. Faith, then, is a trusting in the love and mercy of God. It is hoping for an unseen mercy; it is a conviction that God desires to bless us (Heb. 11:1).

There is something in the heart of all givers, and in God's heart in particular, that recoils at the prospect of a precious gift being refused. Just as my mother would be offended if I declined her offer of an inheritance, so God is offended if we refuse to believe that he is merciful and loving enough to give us good gifts, in spite of ourselves. The writer of Hebrews captures this thought in 11:6, "And without faith it is impossible to please him, for whoever would draw near to God must believe that he exists and that he rewards those who seek him."

In order to find ourselves in the enviable position of "pleasing God," we must have a faith that believes that the invisible God is really and truly here, and that he'll reward our seeking of him; that was all that was required of the Israelite children and that's all that's required of us.

> We shall have a complete definition of faith if we say that it is a firm and sure knowledge of God's favour towards us, based on the truth of a free promise in Christ. . . . We are drawn to seek God when we are told that our safety is treasured up in him; we are confirmed in this when he declares that he takes a deep interest in our welfare. . . . It would be useless to know that God is true, if he

did not lovingly draw us to himself. We could not lay hold of his mercy, if he did not offer it.[3]

But My Wound Is Too Great

Let's return again to our little one in the desert. What if she spent her last moments looking at her wound and thinking how terrible it was? What if she kept examining it, thinking that it would never get better, believing that she deserved to die because she had grumbled against God along with her parents? What if she kept waiting for it to get better before she looked up because she knew she wasn't worthy of healing? She would have died looking at herself. Like the Old Testament leper Naaman,[4] if she thought her wounds were too serious to be so easily healed she would miss God's gracious gift. This is the downfall of everyone who sees their failures as being greater than God's grace.

Look up from your reading again and focus on that other object for a moment. When you looked away you couldn't read this page, could you? In the same way, the Lord calls us to fasten our eyes on him and not on all the sinful toxins in our heart (Isa. 45:22; Mic. 7:7).[5] We're invited to look away from ourselves and our great need and to focus on his overflowing bounty, or as A. W. Tozer plainly advised, "Stop tinkering with your soul and look away to the perfect One."[6]

My Wound Isn't All That Bad

I can imagine another child in the wilderness, perhaps an older one, thinking that God's answer for her was ridiculous. Upon hearing of God's invitation through Moses, perhaps she scoffed and continued to try to improve her condition on her own. Maybe she thought she really wasn't all that sick. Perhaps she assumed that since she hadn't complained all that much, the snake's bite would only make her unwell and not actually kill her. This is the downfall of everyone who thinks their sins are insignificant and God's grace in Christ is an overreaction. She'll die in the wasteland, too. Like Nicodemus, many of us need our self-confidence and self-reliance annihilated before we're willing to look to him in faith and to believe.

It's easy to see why Paul said that the cross is a stumbling block to the self-righteous religious and foolishness to the hedonistic irreligious (1 Cor. 1:23), isn't it? Whether we're overly introspective and excessively aware of our failures or blindly proud and self-sufficient, the gospel dares us to look away to Another in faith.

His Eyes Seeking Yours

What will you discover when you turn your eyes in dependence upon the Lord? You'll find him gazing back at you, eagerly waiting to bless. Jesus has given us a wonderful example of the Father's keen watchfulness in Luke 15. Upon tiring of fighting with pigs for food, the Prodigal Son had finally "come to himself" and begun the journey home. I'm sure that as he walked, he searched intently for some sign of his house in the distance. But he wasn't the only one who was seeking:

> He arose and came to his father. *But while he was still a long way off, his father saw him and felt compassion, and ran and embraced him and kissed him.* And the son said to him, "Father, I have sinned against heaven and before you. I am no longer worthy to be called your son." But the father said to his servants, "Bring quickly the best robe, and put it on him, and put a ring on his hand, and shoes on his feet. And bring the fattened calf and kill it, and let us eat and celebrate. For this my son was dead, and is alive again; he was lost, and is found." And they began to celebrate. (Luke 15:20–24)

Isn't that a glorious depiction of God's gracious stance toward us? While we're still far away, his compassion overwhelms him and *he* runs toward *us*! He is not standing around, waiting for us to grovel and prove that we're properly sorry. He doesn't allow us to come to him as hired servants (v. 19). No, if we're going to return to him, then he is going to enjoy the pleasure of graciously blessing us with all the riches of full sonship. He loves to be generous to the undeserving. What do we need to say to him when we return? Simply, "I've sinned and I'm not worthy of your blessings on my own. But I'm trusting that you're as merciful as you say you are."

"For the eyes of the LORD run to and fro throughout the whole earth, to give strong support to those whose heart is blameless toward him" (2 Chron. 16:9). God is seeking out, looking for every eye turned in faith toward him. What is this "blamelessness" that God loves to bless? Is it a perfect record of disciplined righteousness? No. It's simple reliance on him and a turning away from all other sources of support (see 2 Chron. 16:7–9). It's believing that the righteousness God requires has to be pursued by faith and not by our own efforts (Rom. 9:32).

God delights in proving himself strong on behalf of all who throw themselves unreservedly onto his mercy. He doesn't frown at you when you recognize your neediness and cry out in faith for help. No, he revels in his mercy and grace being known and boasted about by you. "And because of him you are in Christ Jesus, who became to us wisdom from God, righteousness and sanctification and redemption, so that, as it is written, '*Let the one who boasts, boast in the Lord*'" (1 Cor. 1:30–31).

It's just like the Lord to make faith as easy as a simple glance, isn't it? Salvation (and all the riches that accompany it) should require Herculean effort on our part—a jumping up into heaven to bring Christ down to us or a leap into the abyss to bring him back from death. But that's not what saving faith is. No,

"The word is near you, *in your mouth* and *in your heart*" (that is, the word of faith that we proclaim); because, if you confess with your mouth that Jesus is Lord and believe in your heart that God raised him from the dead, you will be saved. For with the heart one believes and is justified, and with the mouth one confesses and is saved. For the Scripture says, "*Everyone who believes in him will not be put to shame*." For there is no distinction between Jew and Greek; for the same Lord is Lord of all, *bestowing his riches on all who call on him*. For "everyone who calls on the name of the Lord will be saved." (Rom. 10:8–13)

We don't need any great strength, wisdom, or skill to breathe out a word, do we? Doesn't it seem as though what he has asked us to do should be easily within everyone's capacity? As he tells us that the "word of faith" we need is as close to us as our own heart, we should at least be able to breathe it out, shouldn't we? But the truth is that because of sin's poison, we're so weak and helpless we can't accomplish even the most simple task; on our own we're simply unable to believe.

The Gift of God

Like the little one who was so ill from the serpent's bite that she was unable even to turn her eyes towards God's promised deliverance, we're faced with a dreadful dilemma. We're told that great riches await us when we look to him in faith, but we're unable to accomplish even as simple a motion as this. And so he again reveals his overwhelming compassion and provides for us what we cannot provide for ourselves. He gives us the gift of saving faith. "For by grace you have been saved through faith. *And this is not your own doing; it is the gift of God*" (Eph. 2:8).

Leaving nothing to our abilities, Jesus himself initiates our faith, and he'll oversee it to its perfect completion. We're to rely totally on him, the "one on whom (our) faith depends from beginning to end" (see Heb. 12:2).[7]

The Sum of Our Belief

What do you and I need to believe? We need to believe what the Israelites and the Prodigal Son believed: that we're in desperate poverty of soul, but God is merciful and good, and that if we look to him, he'll supply everything we truly need. If we simply lift our eyes in response to his invitation, we shall live.

We will live because we will be freed from the curse that rested on us as lawbreakers. We will inherit the blessings of those who live by faith—faith that believes that Christ bore the curse, indeed, became the curse in our place, and that the righteousness required by a holy God has been granted to us. All of this is given to us solely on the basis of his gracious gift made effectual by faith (see Gal. 3:10–14).

The only condition on which Christ's righteousness is accredited to us is faith in him. What was revealed to Paul and what later consoled Martin Luther's burdened conscience was this simple fact: "The just shall live by faith" (Rom. 1:17 NKJV). What does this simple statement mean? What do I need to know? Only that I am to believe the gospel truth of justification:

> Even though my conscience accuses me of having grievously sinned against all of God's commandments and of never having kept any of them, and even though I am inclined toward all evil, nevertheless, without my deserving it at all, out of sheer grace, God grants and credits to me the perfect satisfaction, righteousness, and holiness of Christ, as if I had never sinned nor been a sinner, as if I had been as perfectly obedient as Christ was obedient for me. All I need to do is to accept the gift of God with a believing heart.[8]

We don't have to have a great faith; we're just commanded to believe that God will do what he says he will do. What is this faith we need? It's the assurance that God is too good to lie to us, and that if we answer the call to come to him he will never cast us out (John 6:37).

GROWING YOUR FAITH

Even though the *amount* of faith we have cannot make us any more or less justified, the strength of our faith will grow in direct proportion to our exposure to God's Word, particularly as it highlights God's love for us in the gospel.

As we think on our sweet relationship with him, we'll find joyful gratitude and humble confidence blossoming within our hearts. For instance, we'll grow in our belief that he really is good and that we don't have to fear obedience (1 Pet. 3:6), because he loves us too much to command anything that will ultimately harm us. We'll no longer be driven to protect our selfish interests, because we'll see that he has given us an interest in Christ, and Christ is presenting our needs before his Father at every moment. The pride and arrogance that once commandeered our souls will be crushed beneath Golgotha's blood-soaked mount, as we perceive who we really are and what we truly deserve. Anger and bitterness will be put away because we'll remember that we've been forgiven by God for Christ's sake (Eph. 4:32) so we don't have to fight for our rights. As we pursue an ever-growing understanding of the Lord, his gracious character and our need to rely completely on him, the motivation to respond in grateful obedience will grow within us (Matt. 13:18ff.).

Consider the following verses about the gospel and notice how the Spirit enlightens and strengthens our faith. What benefits are ours through hearing the Word about Christ?

• "So faith comes from hearing, and hearing through the word of Christ." (Rom. 10:17)

• "It was before your eyes that Jesus Christ was publicly portrayed as crucified. Let me ask you only this: Did you receive the Spirit by works of the law or by hearing with faith? . . . Does he who supplies the Spirit to you and works miracles among you do so by works of the law, or by hearing with faith?" (Gal. 3:1–2, 5)

• "For I am not ashamed of the gospel, for it is the power of God for salvation to everyone who believes." (Rom. 1:16)

• "For the word of the cross is folly to those who are perishing, but to us who are being saved it is the power of God." (1 Cor. 1:18)

• "You have heard before in the word of the truth, the gospel, which has come to you, as indeed in the whole world it is bearing fruit and growing—as it also does among you, since the day you heard it and understood the grace of God in truth." (Col. 1:5–6)

• "Like newborn infants, long for the pure spiritual milk, that by it you may grow up into salvation— if indeed you have tasted that the Lord is good." (1 Pet. 2:2–3)

All true Christians want to mature in their salvation. We all want to bear fruit and grow. We want to experience the powerful work of the Spirit in our lives to free us from sin, and we look forward to the day when we hear those blessed words, "Well done, good and faithful servant."

But we also struggle in a fierce and constant battle against our sinful nature, our fundamental unbelief, our selfish desires enflamed by the world's lies, and the fiery darts of the evil one. God's answer to these struggles is simple: we are to arm ourselves with truth and the breastplate of righteousness. We're to protect our steps with the ready response that flows from the gospel of peace. In "all" circumstances we're to "take up the shield of faith" with which we'll "extinguish all the flaming darts of the evil one," just as the sting of the fiery serpents' bite was cured in the wilderness. We're to guard our minds with thoughts of our salvation, and then we're to fight with courage against the evil we face every day with the sword of the Spirit, the Word of God (see Eph. 6:13–18).

How does this happen? Of course, it happens by God's glorious grace, but it is a grace that calls us to look to him in belief and gratitude, to believe that we will ultimately triumph over sin because he has promised to complete his work in us. He is calling us to faith. Will you lift your eyes to him today? Will you transfer all your trust to him and believe that the One who did not withhold his only Son from you will also freely give you all good things? The loving Savior who hung on Calvary's tree for Nicodemus and gave him faith to believe is seeking your uplifted eyes. Look to him; believe in his loving provision and live.

REALIZING HOW GOD'S LOVE TRANSFORMS YOUR IDENTITY AND LIFE

1) Consider God's kindness in giving us the visible symbols of the cross and the serpent on the pole that point out invisible truths. He does so to assure and encourage us. Can you think of any other visible symbols of invisible realities in which we're called to witness the gospel? Why do you think God is so careful to assure us?

2) A. W. Tozer wrote, "Faith is the gaze of the soul upon a saving God. . . . Faith is the least self-regarding of the virtues. It is by its very nature scarcely conscious of its own existence. Like the eye which sees everything in front of it and never sees itself, faith is occupied with the Object upon which it rests and pays no attention to itself at all."[9] Does this definition of faith differ from what you've previously thought? How?

3) The sole condition for your new righteous identity is faith in the Lord Jesus Christ. Faith is simply an instrument by which you appropriate Christ and his righteousness. See Romans 1:17; 3:25–26; 4:20, 22; Philippians 3:8–11; Galatians 2:16. Does this understanding of faith encourage you? Why or why not?

4) Do you see that faith is simply a matter of believing that God is as loving as he claims to be? In what ways do you disbelieve? Have you ever wondered at his dealings with you or accused him of unkindness? What does the gospel tell you about this way of thinking?

5) Summarize in four or five sentences what you've learned from this chapter.

PART TWO

HOW GOD'S LOVE
TRANSFORMS OUR LIFE

CHAPTER SEVEN

BE WHO YOU ARE

*If then you have been raised with Christ, seek the things that are
above, where Christ is, seated at the right hand of God.*

COLOSSIANS 3:1

In the preceding six chapters, you've been given a fresh reminder
of God's astounding love for you in Christ and how important it
is to remember his love every single day. We've seen how verses like
John 3:16 can lose their power to motivate and transform, especially as we get caught up in the struggle to live a godly life. We've
discussed how devaluing the gospel results in a spiritual blindness
that can stunt growth (2 Pet. 1:9) and how many of us function
from day to day as foster children rather than well-loved sons and
daughters.

In this chapter, we're going to be shifting our study from looking primarily at how God's love transforms us at the level of our
identity to how it transforms our daily life. If, in your heart you just
said, "Ah, finally!" please remember that your growth in holiness
is firmly bound to your appreciation of the gospel and God's love,
*for it is only an appreciation of his love that can motivate genuine
obedience*. Outward obedience can be and frequently is generated
by other motives, such as the fear of failure or desire for approval,
but this kind of obedience (which isn't obedience at all) only results
in pride, despair, or self-indulgence and, because it is done out of
love for self, more sin.

THE INDICATIVE AND THE IMPERATIVE . . . *WHAT*?

What we're going to discuss now can be summarized in the simple phrase "Be who you are." When theologians talk about the two categories we're about to discuss, sometimes they use these words: the *indicative* and the *imperative*. Because I think that these words will be helpful for our study, let me define them for you. When I use the term *indicative* I'm talking about what has already been indicated or declared about you. The indicative informs us of an accomplished fact. Here's an indicative statement: "God in Christ has forgiven you."

On the other hand, the *imperative* comes to us in the form of a command or direction. In Ephesians 4:32, Paul gives us this command: "Be kind to one another, tenderhearted, forgiving one another." The New Testament is filled with the imperative: we're commanded to live changed lives.

The beautiful balance between the indicative (who you are in Christ) and the imperative (who you're becoming in Christ) is perfectly demonstrated in the verse we've been considering. The entire verse reads, "Be kind to one another, tenderhearted, forgiving one another, *as* God in Christ forgave you." Can you see how the imperative, "Be kind, tenderhearted and forgiving," is firmly anchored in the indicative, "you're forgiven in Christ"? This verse demonstrates a beautiful synergy that not only tells us what to do, but also plants within our souls the only motive that will empower God-pleasing compliance: what God has already done. We've *already* been forgiven in Christ. So many of us cavalierly gloss over what he has done and zero in on what we're to do, and that shift, though it might seem slight, makes all the difference in the world. Our obedience has its origin in God's prior action, and forgetting that truth results in self-righteousness, pride, and despair.

In some cases, the New Testament writers couple indicative statements with both negative and positive imperatives, in other words, commands to stop doing one thing and to start doing another. For instance, we might read this kind of a statement:

Because such-and-such is true about you (the indicative), you should put off this kind of behavior (the negative imperative) and put on this kind of behavior in its place (the positive imperative). Let me give you an example of this from Colossians 3:

> If then you have been raised with Christ [the indicative], seek the things that are above, where Christ is, seated at the right hand of God. Set your minds on things that are above [a positive imperative], not on things that are on earth [a negative imperative]. For you have died, and your life is hidden with Christ in God. When Christ who is your life appears, then you also will appear with him in glory [the indicative]. Put to death therefore what is earthly in you [a negative imperative]. . . . Put on then [a positive imperative], as God's chosen ones, holy and beloved [the indicative], compassionate hearts, kindness, humility, meekness, and patience, bearing with one another and, if one has a complaint against another, forgiving each other [a positive imperative]; as the Lord has forgiven you [the indicative], so you also must forgive [a positive imperative]. (vv. 1–5, 12–13)

Through the use of this indicative/imperative paradigm, I trust that the relationship between who you already are and how he has called you to live has become clearer to you and that it will be a tool you'll be able to use as you study Scripture in the future.

Gospel-Driven Imperatives

I've spent a great deal of time reminding you of what God in his love has already accomplished in you. I've purposely done this because I think that's where most serious Christians fail; and because they fail to hold close these marvelous truths, their obedience becomes a burdensome exercise in self-improvement. But this focus on what the gospel declares about you doesn't mean in any sense that your thoughts of the gospel must end there, in mere inactive thought. In fact, those who would focus exclusively on pondering the gospel and "preclude all activity and commend passivity are in error."[1] They're in error because they must ignore much of the plain teaching of Scripture.

The point here is that the indicative does not describe a reality that
exists by itself, one to which a heart for the imperative [automatically]
. . . follows as a subsequent, presumably detachable addition.[2]

We cannot assume that a constant consideration of the gospel
will automatically eventuate in holy living, or why would the writers
of the New Testament, men whose lives were robustly tethered to the
gospel, have written so much by way of the imperative? The wonderful pronouncements God has made about us cannot and must not be
disconnected from the wonderful expectations he has of us.[3] In other
words, *gospel-declaration must not be severed from gospel-obligation*. Not that we must now throw away all thought of God's grace
and "get to work." No, but neither should we throw away all thought
of our obligations to ponder his declarations only. The full teaching of
the New Testament seems plain on this topic: the declarations of the
gospel are unavoidably tied to the obligations of the gospel.

I've told you that both gospel-declarations (indicatives) and
gospel-obligations (imperatives) are essential to our growth in
becoming the people we already are. Let me give you two examples
of how this truth might play out in our daily lives.

Obligation without Declaration

In my experience, this is where most serious-minded believers get off
track. In our desire to live lives that are pleasing to God, it's easy to
forget that sanctification (our change into Christlikeness) is, as the
Westminster Divines wrote, "an act of God's grace."[4] It is an act of
God's grace because his work *in* us is prior to anything holy blossoming *from* us, either from our actions or the motives that prompt them.
Our obedience is *entirely* the result of the seed he has planted in us
and the work of the Spirit through us. I doubt that many of us would
disagree with this statement in theory, but I wonder if we embrace it
as intentionally as we should. Our sanctification is from God alone
who has "made us pure and holy" (1 Cor. 1:30 NLT) through Jesus
Christ. "God's work in salvation . . . never absorbs or invalidates
man's work, but arouses and stimulates it and gives it meaning."[5]

A skewed perspective on God's activity in our sanctification will result in an overemphasis on outward conformity to the imperatives. It will breed one of two categories of moralism. The first is what I'm calling the Happy Moralist.[6]

The Happy Moralist is the person who thinks that his holiness rests pretty much on his own efforts but isn't worried because he has reduced God's demands for outward conformity to simplistic rules like *don't drink, don't chew, don't run with them that do*, or any of a thousand outward commands that don't engage the heart. If avoiding certain external behaviors, "Do not handle, do not taste, do not touch,"[7] is all God demands of us, then we can be happy with our righteousness and, while we're at it, it'll be easy to be judgmental and look down on others, too.

Of course, the problem that the Happy Moralist must face is that all of his conformity to mere external regulations is of "no value in stopping the indulgence of the flesh" (Col. 2:23). The sinful heart is never transformed by conformity to the imperatives but only by relationship with the One who cleanses hearts. All of the Happy Moralist's external law keeping doesn't touch the source of his sin—the desires of his heart. In fact, his self-styled successes only serve to make him blind to his weaknesses and proud of his accomplishments. The rich young ruler was a Happy Moralist until he met the Christ who decimated his self-esteem and showed him his need. The self-indulgence that the Happy Moralist will inevitably fall into is simply an outworking of his faltering self-reliance; we can only keep up appearances for so long before we fall. The sole protection against self-indulgence is not to trust in self at all.

Now, let me introduce you to the Sad Moralist. The Sad Moralist is the person who understands the profound depth of God's demands: to love him with all that we are, to love our neighbors as ourselves. He sees that true holiness is not a matter of mere externals, and in this he is right; but he is also crushed by the depth of his inability to even begin to achieve the righteousness God requires. His conscience always accuses him, he wonders about his salvation, he is over-punctilious about every thought, scrupulous to a fault; he rehearses his failures over and over in his mind, is overwrought with guilt, and wonders about the joy and rest other Christians seem to have. And "instead of examining himself for biblical signs of regeneration through possession of simple faith, he ransack[s] his heart for foolproof signs of advanced holiness."[8] "Joy? How could I be joyful?" he wonders. "How could I laugh when I've fallen so far short . . . when my awareness of my failures and obligations are annihilating me?"

Like the Happy Moralist, this unhappy soul will continually be tempted to fall into self-indulgence, perhaps by spending hours and hours in introspection, self-recrimination, and what might be called depression or anxiety. He'll compare his walk with others, and instead of looking down on them, he'll look down on himself. He is the overwrought Christian who claims to know God's grace but never finds the freedom to serve Christ from grateful obedience, because he believes his obedience is never perfect enough. He needs to see that Jesus is greater than his sin, greater than his opinion of himself. He needs the humility that a true embracing of utter depravity brings and the reassurance that a true embracing of God's sovereignty over his sanctification produces.

The only insurance against man-centered bootstrap sanctification is an "exultant faith which thrives on God alone and 'forgets not all of his benefits.'"[9] Both the happy and the sad moralist must continually focus and refocus their life on the benefits the Lord has given then in Christ.

Declaration without Obligation

In contrast to these moralists, the libertine is the Christian who's heard something of God's grace in Christ but hasn't grasped the fact that God's grace, when it's really there, *will* eventuate in a changed life. It's to this person that Paul wrote that the grace of God trains us to "renounce ungodliness and worldly passions, and to live self-controlled, upright, and godly lives in the present age." We're "waiting for our blessed hope, the appearing of the glory of our great God and Savior Jesus Christ, who gave himself for us to redeem us from all lawlessness and to purify for himself a people for his own possession who are *zealous for good works*" (Titus 2:12–14).

The grace of God trains us to renounce ungodliness, live temperate, godly lives, and be zealous for good works. Yes, God rules sovereignly, and in the life of his beloved ones he rules with sovereign grace, mercy, and love. But we mustn't assume that his grace trumps the expectation that we should be holy, for he is holy and his Holy Spirit indwells us. Yes, God is sovereign over our sanctification, but recognition of that truth doesn't excuse us from zealously pursuing it.

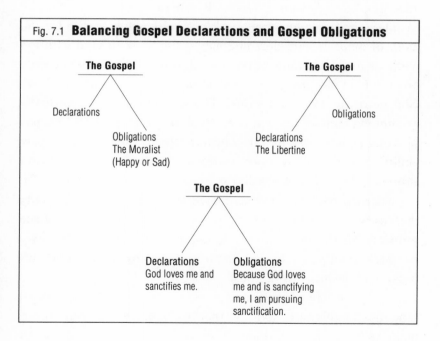

Fig. 7.1 **Balancing Gospel Declarations and Gospel Obligations**

Keeping Declaration and Obligation Together

Here's another one of those indicative/imperative passages that makes clear the delightful synergy we've been discussing. See if you can pick out the declarations and obligations:

Therefore, my beloved, as you have always obeyed, so now, not only as in my presence but much more in my absence, work out your own salvation with fear and trembling, for it is God who works in you, both to will and to work for his good pleasure. (Phil. 2:12–13)

The imperative, "work out your own salvation with fear and trembling," is framed by and anchored to the indicative, "for it is God who works in you, both to will and to work for his good pleasure." Let me reiterate that we must firmly hold to the truth that God's command to "work" is impossible to obey unless he has already worked in us the desire to work—the "willing"—and the ability to work—the "doing"—but the command to work is there, nevertheless.

Here, quite plainly, "the work of God is the incentive for the work of man."[10] Paul doesn't contrast the work of God with the work of man, but rather says that all our work is possible *only* because God has *already* worked in us. So, who's working? Does God work or does man work? The answer, in accord with the astounding logic of heaven, is a resounding yes! Because God has said that he has given us a new heart with new motives and a new ability to work, we are wholeheartedly to pursue holiness, always assuming that it is God's will that we obey him. In saying this, I'm not asserting that we work separately from God's work, but only that, as we rest in the work he has done, we consider and pursue seriously all the imperatives. Again, we know that we'll never complete them perfectly, and that if we have any success at all, it's because of his *prior* work in us.

This perspective frees us and gives us confidence in our eventual sanctification because God says that he continues to, by his Spirit, make us both willing and able to do the good he has ordained for us to do.[11] This is what it means to walk by faith and not by sight (2 Cor. 5:7). My faith tells me that *Christ is in me.* I am assured that the resurrected, ascended Lord dwells right now within my mortal body, and therefore I have the confidence I need to continue to pursue imitation of the unseen Christ. Even though my obedience is not perfect and my motives are never completely pure, I still believe that the faltering baby steps I'm taking are caused by him and pleasing to him. Because he has conquered death and sin and is ruling and overruling in every facet of my life, I have faith to seek conformity to gospel obligations that my new identity presses upon me.

Paul ends one of the most blatantly gospel-exalting passages in the New Testament, Ephesians 2:1–9,[12] with an interesting statement. He has just described God's grace and our inability to save ourselves, when he writes, "We are his workmanship, created in Christ Jesus for good works, which God prepared beforehand, that we should walk in them" (Eph. 2:10).

Here we are again with both declarations and obligations, indicatives and imperatives. Our union with Christ Jesus is his project, his workmanship, his work. He has done everything that needs to be done to secure our relationship to himself. But that's not all he's done. He has also already prepared good works for us to do, to "walk in." The comforting truth is that even here, when the onus should be entirely on us, he has taken care of this, too. We will complete the good he has obligated us to complete *because he has already completed it.* Again, that doesn't mean that we sit around, waiting for the Lord to lift our hand to do what he wants, any more than we wait to pray until he physically opens our mouth and breathes air through our vocal chords. What it does mean, though, is that we can be courageous in our faith—we can boldly pursue godly living because he has made us able to do so.

Another passage that clearly demonstrates this relationship of God's work and man's work is 1 Corinthians 15:10: "But by the grace of God I am what I am, and his grace toward me was not in vain. On the contrary, I worked harder than any of them, though it was not I, but the grace of God that is with me." Paul says that he worked harder than any of the other apostles. It was actually Paul who preached, who traveled, who suffered hardship. But it was also the grace of God in him that was motivating and energizing the work. Again, here's our question: Who works: God or us? Paul said that he "worked harder" than anyone else but knew that it was really "the grace of God" that was working through him.

This is our hope, and it's not some pathetic wish. It's a joyful confidence in his power to transform. In fact, he is so sure of our sanctification that he speaks of it as though it had already happened: "We *have been* sanctified through the offering of the body of Jesus Christ once for all" (Heb. 10:10; see also 1 Cor. 1:2, 30; 6:11). God's purpose in our redemption isn't simply our justification; it is our complete transformation. We who are justified *will* be sanctified.

Our Hope: The Seed Will Produce Fruit

Progressive sanctification, that slow process of change into Christlikeness, means, in its simplest form, that what we've already been made to be *in Christ* (our justification), we are growing to be *in our practice* (our sanctification).

This sanctification is nothing less than a guaranteed blossoming of the gospel seed that has been implanted within the soul of every born-again believer (1 Pet. 1:23–25). It is not imitation of a personality alien to us, but rather it is the inward renovation of our souls by the power of the resurrected Christ who resides *within* us. Imagine a natural seed within your heart invisibly germinating, and then extending its tender roots, branching out and growing stronger, becoming more and more entrenched until it finally fills your entire soul. That's what the seed of the gospel is like within you; it *will* reproduce the image of Jesus.

Without faith that this seed will change us, we may be tempted to become discouraged and give up, because all we see is our body, which is wasting away, and the powerful influence of our old nature. But rather than being overwhelmed and ultimately crushed by our weaknesses, failures, and doubts, our faith informs us of this truth: "Though our outer self is wasting away, *our inner self is being renewed day by day*" (2 Cor. 4:16). Our outer nature is really and truly rotting away, but there is another more significant truth that we must grasp by faith: We *are* being changed; our inner person is being renewed. This new life within us, this new nature, this powerful seed, *will* ripen into a transformed person that accurately reflects his image (Rom. 8:30). How can we be sure that this will happen? Because the *resurrected Christ* guarantees it! He has gone before us as the firstfruits of a harvest that he is presenting to the Lord of the Harvest. "Christ became what we are and then made himself the firstfruits of all that *we will become.*"[13]

Just as the Lord spoke over his creation and decreed that everything would bring forth fruit after its own kind (Gen. 1:11ff.), he has spoken over our life: it is impossible that we should have his life dwelling within us and have no sign of life change. This change may be minuscule, indeed, but this seed will always produce fruit.[14]

The inevitability of our growth in holiness doesn't mean, though, that we'll be perfect in this life or that our obedience won't be stained in some way by sin. For instance, I can't imagine being aware of personal growth in holiness without—and at the exact same moment of the realization of my success—patting myself on the back and falling into the sin of pride and self-sufficiency. Our good works will always and unfailingly be marred by sin, but we're called to pursue them anyway. Only his works are perfect.

The writers of the Heidelberg Catechism understood the struggles present in our pursuit of holiness. They wrote, "In this life even the holiest have only a small beginning of . . . obedience."[15] Why, then, if even our good works are stained and imperfect should we continue to try to perform them? Why bother? Isn't that just an exercise in futility? No,

> we do good because Christ by his Spirit is also *renewing us to be like himself,* so that in all our living we may show that we are *thankful to God for all that he has done for us,* and so that *he may be praised through us.* And we do good so that *we may be assured of our faith by its fruits,* and so that by our godly living *our neighbors may be won over to Christ.*[16]

Here we're given four reasons to continue to strive against sin and seek to do good works in the grace he supplies through the gospel, even though we'll never be completely successful. Let me rephrase these motives so that you'll be able to easily remember them.

1) *Be who you already are.* Christ has already made you new; walk in this newness. You're in him; his Spirit resides in you. Just as surely as his resurrection was the first fruit of an offering given to God, you're part of that guaranteed harvest. Seek to be who he has made you to be, remembering that he has already assured your growth by ordaining good works for you to perform.

2) *Be thankful for who you already are.* Christ has made you new; let your life overflow with gratitude for his goodness. This gratitude will motivate and purify your response to the obligations he has placed on you. Speaking to yourself about the love he has for you will embolden you to courageously pursue holiness, even when your failure is extensive.

3) *Be assured of who you are.* Christ has already made you new, and your continued growth in holiness will remind you of your new identity. This doesn't mean that our assurance rests on our obedience; no, our assurance must be anchored in the obedience of Christ. Our assurance will grow, though, as we see his sanctifying work in us and look back over our lives. We'll be able to see how his power has transformed us "from one degree of glory to another" as we behold him (2 Cor. 3:18).[17]

4) *Be who you are before others.* Christ has loved you and made you new and his kindness and love to you is such a wonderful gift that it must be shared. Your good works are lights that cannot be hidden, and though you don't do them to enhance your reputation, God does use them to bring new life to others.

Faith Working Through Love

I love my grandchildren. Have I mentioned them before? I look at them and I can see the beginnings of the people they will become. I can see the family resemblance and I can imagine what they'll soon be. They're my darlings.

In a much greater way, your heavenly Father looks at you and sees what you will become. He is not worried about your ultimate success; he is ruling as the sovereign King over your life, making sure you'll become the person he wants you to be.

So, what is the proper response to all these wonderful declarations? Nothing less than grateful obedience or "faith working through love" (Gal. 5:6). Notice that our faith is to work, but it isn't to work through fear of abandonment or out of the desire to prove ourselves. No, our faith works because we love, and we love because he has first loved us. Our faith is then emboldened by this responsive love: we've been loved, we've been assured of our justification; our Father speaks of our sanctification as if it had already occurred. By faith, then, we can courageously pursue growth into our true identity. The Father has gone before us, and the God-Man, Jesus Christ, has paved the road and cleared all obstacles out of the way. The first offering has been offered, guaranteeing that the rest of the harvest is on its way. It cannot fail.

LIVING AND WORKING IN THE LIGHT OF THE GOSPEL

I recently had a conversation with a Christian friend who asked me if I was presently involved in a book project. "Yes," I replied, "I'm writing about the gospel."

"Which Gospel?" she wondered. "Matthew or John or . . . ?"

"Not on *a* Gospel, on *the* gospel. I'm writing a book about the gospel for people who think they already know it."

An eerie silence descended down over us while a glazed look settled over her eyes. I can't tell you how many times I've had that conversation since I've begun this project. It seems to astonish my peers that I think we need to hear the old news again. So, before we leave this chapter on indicatives and imperatives, here's one final reminder: our glorious new identity in Christ, all the wonderful indicatives in Scripture, must *always* remain the catalyst, motive, and ground for our transformation. This is true first of all, because this is how the Spirit, whose job it is to sanctify us, has structured

Scripture. Trying to disengage our work *for* Christ from our union *with* Christ does violence to the method by which the Spirit has obviously chosen to sanctify us.[18]

Secondly, thinking deeply about the gospel is both necessary and beneficial because we are all so prone to self-sufficiency and self-reliance. The gospel serves us by stripping away vain-glorious delusions we harbor about our innate goodness and ability to please God through our self-generated effort. When I forget that the only way that God could stand to have me in his family was by crushing the Son he loves—that without the perfect record of someone else I could not stand before his judicious holiness, that on my own I do not have within me either the desire or the power to please God—I am tempted to believe that I'm really pretty good. And although I might need a nip or tuck, if I try hard enough, I can accomplish all he has called me to. It's when we forget the gospel, when we think we're not really all that bad, not so much in need, not so far from Christlikeness, that pride, arrogance, and the inevitable guilt crush hope and faith.

Our sanctification is rooted in our union with Christ—how can we truly change if we aren't already truly different? How can we fight to win if he hasn't already fought and won? How can we conquer death and sin if he isn't the resurrected One, who lives within us? Indeed, "the moment we turn aside from Christ in the slightest degree, salvation which rests entirely on him gradually disappears,"[19] and discouragement and condemnation will rule our hearts. So let's not forget what he has done and is doing and then, in faith, work with zeal and joy.

Realizing How God's Love Transforms Your Identity and Life

1) Read Colossians 3:1–5, 12–15 and answer the following:
- What are the declarations God has made about you?
- What are the obligations he has placed upon you?
- When you struggle with your inability to perform these

injunctions, what is your only hope? What do the declarations he has made about you mean when you struggle with sin?

2) In what category do you usually find yourself: the happy moralist, the sad moralist, the apathetic libertine? It might be helpful for you to ask yourself these questions: Do I struggle with self-condemnation? Do I find myself frequently falling into self-indulgence? Do I see fear of failure or laziness in myself? Am I condemning of others? Do I compare myself to others and find myself lacking? Understanding the basis of your unique struggle with sanctification will be helpful.

3) Review the four motives for holy living on page 120. Which one speaks most powerfully to you? What normally motivates you to live a holy life? Do you find yourself motivated by a desire to prove your goodness or by self-promotion (pride and ambition), or are you motivated by faith working through love?

4) Summarize in four or five sentences what you've learned from this chapter.

CHAPTER EIGHT

I WILL CLEANSE YOU

"I will sprinkle clean water on you, and you shall be clean . . . and from all your idols I will cleanse you."

EZEKIEL 36:25

I n the last chapter I introduced indicatives and imperatives, the gospel declarations and obligations given to believers. You'll recall that there are two facets of gospel obligation: the positive and the negative. In this chapter, we'll be focusing on the negative side of our gospel-obligation, or what we might call the "put-offs." Instead of narrowing down our focus to a list of specific sins that need to be put off, we'll be considering a paradigm to use as we attack all our sin by faith. This model will encourage you to look past those outward sins to the unseen sins of the heart that animate them. Then, in chapter 9, we'll look at the positive commands, or the "put-ons."

Before we get started though, let me remind you again that these obligations are anchored in the declarations we discussed in the first section of this book. In Romans, Paul's masterful treatise on the gospel, the first imperative doesn't even appear until chapter 6, and then it's a command to *remember* and *apply*: "You also must *consider* yourselves dead to sin and alive to God in Christ Jesus" (Rom. 6:11). So, let's take a moment to do that.[1]

THINK ABOUT IT: YOU ARE DEAD TO SIN

Because of the Father's work in Christ, our old sinful life is dead; that is, we are no longer under sin's dominion. The church corporately and each of us individually have been given a "new basis for self-judgment."[2] If we are no longer to live in sin, we must "understand [ourselves] by faith."[3] We are dead to sin, and not only are we dead to sin's power, we have also been made alive to God, "having been brought under his dominion. What has taken place once in Christ must thus be actualized in a new way of life. . . . [We] must fight our battle in the certainty that our enemy *has been* overcome."[4] Yes, sin has been overcome, and because of Christ's victory we can war.

This first gospel obligation in Romans is a call to faith, to believe that what he says he has done really has been done. The submissive obedience Paul then calls us to in 6:13, "Present yourselves to God as those who have been brought from death to life," is based on faith in the accomplished fact of the gospel: we're dead to sin and alive to God; we've been set free from slavery to sin and endowed with the ability to submit to him.

What this new life means is that we confidently hope for change. We can fight courageously to put off the sin that still dwells in our mortal bodies. We're not on our own; no, we're in him and he has raised us up out of that desolate tomb of sin and death. He has presented us with him, fully alive in the Father's presence. Although we know that this is true, there may be times, particularly when we're struggling against our sin, that we have trouble believing it. And that's when we have to go back to the command to consider. In other words, we have to get our eyes off our sin and back onto his accomplished work on the cross.

Like the Galatians, we need to be reminded of these truths, especially when we're tempted to fall back into the discouragement that self-righteousness and moralism breeds. Take Paul's personal declarations in Galatians 2:20–21 as your own; apply them by faith to your struggle against sin: "I have been crucified with Christ. It is no longer I who live, but Christ who lives in me. And the life I now live in the flesh I live by faith in the Son of God, who loved me and gave himself for me."

Our old nature has been crucified with him. The person we once were is dead, and our bodies have been indwelt with a different spirit, the Spirit of the Risen Christ. Of course, we must take hold of this by faith again and again, as we stubbornly believe that the Son of God cannot abandon us. He loves us so dearly that he gave his life for us.

THINK ABOUT IT: YOU'RE ALIVE IN CHRIST

This is where we remember one particular aspect of the gospel: the resurrection. If the resurrection didn't actually occur, then Christ isn't alive and his life is not resident within us. If he is not living by his Spirit within us in the here-and-now, we don't possess either the desire or the power we need to put off sin. But because the tomb is empty, we can fight valiantly by faith. We know that his sinless life is even now empowering our sinful flesh; it's resident within us.

When it comes to believing that he rose from the dead, we are, it is true, still walking by faith and not by sight, but we have the reliable testimony of those who actually saw the resurrected Lord to encourage us. We know that their testimony is true because so many of them chose death over the denial of what they had seen. They were willing to sacrifice everything because they had seen something that changed all things. They had seen the resurrected, ascended Lord. So, even while they were being martyred, their testimony remained resolute. "Behold, I see the heavens opened," cried Stephen, "and the Son of Man standing at the right hand of God" (Acts 7:56). Because we are *in Christ* and he has passed through death and is living in unobstructed communion with his Father, our growth in holiness is guaranteed.

As the living Christ sustained these early believers, he is, at this moment, sustaining us. Our faith in the work he has already done and is continuing to do will embolden us to zealously pursue sanctification. "Let believers, therefore, learn to *embrace Him*, not only for justification, but also for sanctification, as He has been given to us for both these purposes."[5] So then, let's embrace him, lean on him, and remember him, especially now as we look more closely at the sin that threatens (but only threatens) to overwhelm us.

The Foundation of All Sin

There is one sin that is at the root of all sin: unbelief. The sin of unbelief is what will consign the most moral among us to hell (John 3:18). This damning unbelief is not simply an atheism but rather a refusal to believe that there is a holy, loving, merciful, and gracious God who has willingly done for us what we could not do for ourselves. And even though we who have saving faith have passed from death to life, from condemnation to justification, fragments of this unbelief still remain. At times we still wonder if he is really there, if he is really good, if his word is really reliable, if he loves us. We wonder if he can make us happy.

To illustrate this, I'll tell you about a problem I had responding in godliness when Phil, my husband, came home early from work and interrupted my writing. I'll admit that I was irritated that I had to stop doing what I was intent on. I didn't yell at him or throw my laptop across the room, but I'm sure he knew that I was unhappy that he had interrupted my train of thought. My problem with Phil's early arrival was, at its core, a problem of *unbelief*. It was a faith problem, because at that moment I simply refused to believe that God loved me and that he was lovingly ruling over my life. I doubted that being interrupted was a good he had planned. I failed to believe that he is kind, wise, and powerful. My primary sin was that I failed to believe that God is good and that his plans for my life are good, too.

In addition, in my unbelief I was taking pleasure in unrighteousness (2 Thess. 2:12). I cherished the thought of living life without God interrupting me or messing about in my affairs. I know that none of us would just come right out and shout, "Stop meddling!" at the Lord, but we frequently say it to those God has placed in our path. "I wish you'd just stay out of my way. I have to get this done!"

In taking such pleasure in unrighteousness, I prove myself not only unbelieving but also an idolater. It's not that trying to get my work done is sinful in itself. No, I believe that God has called me to accomplish this task. It becomes sinful when thoughts of an uninterrupted, self-determined day captivate my soul, when accomplishing my goals means more to me than grateful obedience. My plan has become my god; I am an idolater. I worship my idea of a successful day, my right to decree how its every moment will go.

We Are All Worshipers

Unbelief, the primary sin, always breeds idolatry, because we have been created to worship. Our hearts are bent to worship. If you don't think so, just hang around the water cooler at work after an episode of *American Idol* or an NCAA playoff game. People enjoy praising what they love because they are worshipers. *Did you see that basket? Wasn't that the best game ever? She's really got a great voice! I loved listening to her.* These are the words of worshipers.

No one is free from this inclination to worship, not even the person who refuses to worship the living God. No; in fact, someone who refuses to worship God will worship a panoply of gods, because our God-given impulse to worship can only be satiated by God himself. The man who refuses to worship God is doomed to unending thirst, to "the restless futility of bewilderment,"[6] as he frantically searches for true refreshment, hoping to find from things absent what he lacks in things present. He'll be consigned to the worship of a zillion other gods, and yet he still won't be satisfied (Isa. 55:2). The vacuum that is created when we refuse to exclusively devote our worship to the living God is never empty for long. Like mushrooms that pop up overnight in the dark, idols appear instantaneously in the soil of our hearts.

My idolatry on that afternoon when Phil walked in a little early could be called the god of "self," "self-rule," or "freedom from interruption." But in my heart there is a worship driving even those things—the desire for approval. You see, my irritation is a direct result of my worship of other's opinions. I desire to do well at my work so that others will approve of me, and, in turn, I'll approve of myself. I hate being interrupted when I'm "in the groove" because I value the worship and accolades of others. When I put my little irritation in this light, can you see how appalling it truly is?

Fig. 8.1 **Worship God or Worship Idols**

Worship God	**Worship Idols**
Focusing on God's love for us in Christ produces love, joy, peace—more worship for him.	Neglecting his love and goodness produces idolatry, apathy, and a wandering heart, which produces: pride, self-pity, worry, anger, fear, self-indulgence, laziness, more dissatisfaction

---

As bleak a picture as I've painted so far, there are more mushrooms flourishing in the dark recesses of my heart. There are little ones growing around the stalk of what can be called my ruling motivations or idols—the garden-variety sins in my life. These sins are anger, self-pity, worry, fear, self-indulgence, dishonesty, laziness, and, of course, pride.

Fig. 8.2 **Unbelief Breeds Idolatry and Sin**

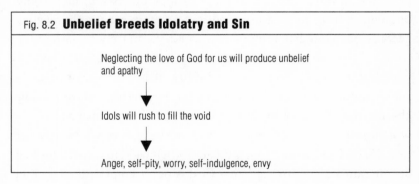

Neglecting the love of God for us will produce unbelief and apathy

▼

Idols will rush to fill the void

▼

Anger, self-pity, worry, self-indulgence, envy

I realize that thinking about unbelief and idolatry producing other sins might be new to you, so let me give you two examples of this principle from Scripture: one from our Lord and one from the senior pastor of the church in Jerusalem, James.

WHERE IS YOUR TREASURE?

In the Sermon on the Mount, Jesus taught his followers how to overcome sinful fear and worry. His advice was not simply, "Do not be anxious," although he did say that (Matt. 6:25). Instead, he traced our problem with worry back to the treasure chest of our hearts, back to the locus of our worship—our unbelief and idolatry. He said:

> Do not lay up for yourselves treasures on earth, where moth and rust destroy and where thieves break in and steal, but lay up for yourselves treasures in heaven, where neither moth nor rust destroys and where thieves do not break in and steal. For where your treasure is, there your heart will be also. . . . Therefore . . . do not be anxious. (Matt. 6:19–21, 25)

If we treasure, value, and love anything more than his kingdom and his righteousness, we'll be forced into slavish fear and beset with worry. Why? Because we live in a sin-cursed, fallen world. Our stocks fall, our computers fritz-out, our children rebel, churches implode, people we love leave, our bodies betray us; life is out of our control. Thieves, moths, and rust run rampant. It doesn't take long for our children to learn that it's a dangerous world out there! And if our treasure is out there, at the mercy of sinful people and a fallen creation, it's at risk, we're at risk, and we'd better worry.

Can you see how a simple command to simply stop worrying isn't enough? Our worry is the result of other grave sins: unbelief and idolatry. Until those sins are dealt with, we'll never get at the real causes of our anxieties.

When we fail to value the real treasure that has been deposited in our hearts, in these "jars of clay," the door will open to other seductive treasures that insist upon a place in our hearts and create fear and terror at the possibility of loss. But when the gospel message of the "light of the knowledge of the glory of God [seen] in the face of Jesus Christ" (2 Cor. 4:6) captivates us as it should, all our worst fears are calmed by the overwhelming brilliance of his presence. When he is our treasure, when we believe that his love has been set on us, then worries about success and failure, gain and loss, will diminish drastically.

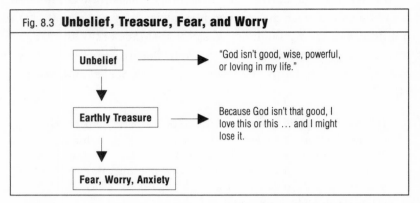

Fig. 8.3 **Unbelief, Treasure, Fear, and Worry**

Unbelief → "God isn't good, wise, powerful, or loving in my life."

Earthly Treasure → Because God isn't that good, I love this or this ... and I might lose it.

Fear, Worry, Anxiety

What was Jesus' answer to our unbelief, idolatry, and resultant fears and worries that plague us? He answered with gospel-declarations: we don't have to live like foster children; we have a Father who loves us and will provide all we need (Matt. 6:26, 30, 32); we're his, and all that he has given to the Son, the Son has shared with us (1 Cor. 3:21–23). Right now and forever we will always have all we need.

To war against our worries, then, we must treasure him and make him the sun around which our thoughts and affections track. When he is there at the center of our devotion, we'll no longer fear loss; moths, rust, and thieves are barred from the sacred inner vault where his glory shines brightly. But we'll never treasure him if we don't consciously think on him, on his love, on the gospel. Simply put, *we worry because we don't spend enough time treasuring what he has already done.* Thoughts of his love for us in Christ will assure us of what he will do for us in our daily lives. Think of it: he didn't withhold his beloved Son from us, so shouldn't we rely fully on him to help us live for him today?

Furthermore, because of the Father's adopting love, we are freed from worry's fruit: envy, stinginess, ruthless ambition, and self-protection. We can be generous, we can rejoice in others' successes, and we can live at peace because we've experienced him and learned that his glory is where real treasure is. We don't have to war to build our own kingdom and establish our own righteousness because we've already been generously lavished with both in Christ. And when we consider this, we'll be satisfied with him and motivated to seek his kingdom and his righteousness instead of our own.

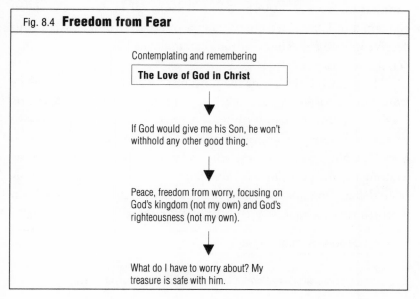

Fig. 8.4 **Freedom from Fear**

Contemplating and remembering

The Love of God in Christ

If God would give me his Son, he won't withhold any other good thing.

Peace, freedom from worry, focusing on God's kingdom (not my own) and God's righteousness (not my own).

What do I have to worry about? My treasure is safe with him.

THE DESIRES THAT RULE OUR SOULS

In the same way, James warns us about our treasures, those desires or "passions" that are at war within us. He writes:

> What is the source of quarrels and conflicts among you? Is not the source your pleasures that wage war in your members? You lust and do not have; so you commit murder. You are envious and cannot obtain; so you fight and quarrel. You do not have because you do not ask. You ask and do not receive, because you ask with wrong motives, so that you may spend it on your pleasures. (James 4:1-3 NASB)

When James speaks of our "passions," he is using a strong term that means "sensual delight," "desire,"[7] "to covet," "to long for" and "to lust after."[8] James doesn't tell us, "Learn to communicate your needs more clearly," nor does he say, "Your problem with anger and conflict is that you're task-oriented." No, he says our anger and conflicts are a gospel problem. We are, in his words, "adulterous people" (4:4). Why? Because although we've been betrothed to Christ, we are chasing around after other lovers who deceive us into believing that they can make us happy. This is unbelief and idolatry.

The gospel declarations the Lord has made are meant to free us from our never-ending craving for more. Because he has made us his own and given us everything in Christ, we don't have to shove others aside, envy them, fight with them, or murder them. We've got something better: a God who delights in drawing near to us, exalting us, and granting us grace (James 4:6–8). The gospel frees us from demanding our own way, because nothing we desire to obtain is worth sinning against such love and kindness.

Fig. 8.5 **Freedom from Anger**

Loving Anything More Than We Love God (spiritual adultery)

Anger, conflict, envy, dissatisfaction, sinful prayers, greed, pride, God's resistance

Because We've Been So Loved

Grace, peace, humility, courage

Our Search for Happiness

Whether our treasured idol is comfort, romance, respect, security, or significance, we worship these false gods because we believe that if we obtained them, we'd finally be happy. This desire for happiness is universal. Everyone is looking for that one person, position, or possession that they hope will make them at last and completely satisfied. We're all seeking the secret that will transport our lives into a perpetual beer commercial where we sit around a comfy campfire and muse with our pals: "It doesn't get any better than this."

Contrary to what many people assume, I don't believe that the Bible teaches that there is anything wrong with this desire to be happy. As a matter of fact, the Lord uses this desire to motivate us because he promises it as a reward to all who put their trust in him (Ps. 144:15). Our failures don't stem from a lack of desire for happiness. In fact, it is the underlying motive of everything we do. Seventeenth-century Christian philosopher Blaise Pascal wrote, "All look for happiness without exception. Although they use different means, they all strive toward this objective. That is why some go to war and some do other things. So this is the motive for every deed of man, including those who hang themselves."[9]

Our problem is not that we desire happiness. No, our problem is that we continue to foolishly believe that we can attain it apart from him. We think that if we just try hard enough, the next time we'll get it right (whatever *it* is) and we'll be happy. Instead of pushing through to the true source of all joy and happiness, we sinfully believe the false promises of lesser gods.

> We are half-hearted creatures, fooling about with drink and sex and ambition when infinite joy is offered us, like an ignorant child who wants to go on making mud pies in a slum because he cannot imagine what is meant by the offer of a holiday at the sea. *We are far too easily pleased.*[10]

Because we've been given something infinitely better—pure joy without regret—we don't have to settle for cheap imitations. When we realize where true happiness comes from, that it won't be found in new and better relationships or things or the comfort, pride, respect, or safety any of these might bring, we can pursue it with the Lord's blessing.

The kind of happiness we long for isn't found in anything here on earth. We've been created for him, and until we're settled on him, we'll always be restless and discontented.[11] Only a deep appreciation of all he has done for us in Christ will motivate us to pursue true happiness, to put off all of our shabby attempts to make our mud pies a little more tasty, and to seek the One who loves us more than we'll ever comprehend.

Seeking Your Happiness in Him

We've begun our discussion of gospel obligations, or negative imperatives, by thinking about how unbelief, idolatry, and the sins that flow from them occur in our hearts. What follows now are a few practical steps to take as you fight by faith for real happiness.

• *Pray that God would reveal your unbelief and idolatry to you.* I know that it's hard to see the sin within our hearts, but the Holy Spirit can bring us conviction and enlightenment. He can reveal the lies we've believed: *If I don't have this I'll never be happy.* He can open our eyes to our functional gods and the unbelief at their core.

• *Prayerfully meditate on Scripture and ask God to apply it to you.* Only the Word of God is able to "discern" the thoughts and intentions of the heart (Heb. 4:12). As you meditate on his word, ask him to apply it personally to you, to help you discern the very motives that compel your sin.

• *Confess any unbelief or idolatry that you're aware of.* Instead of trying to hide or deny idolatry or unbelief, flee to the cross! Your Savior has already borne these sins in your place. He has paid the penalty for them and his resurrection breaks their power in your life. "If we confess our sins, he is faithful and just to forgive us our sins and to cleanse us from all unrighteousness" (1 John 1:9).

• *Ask God to make himself your chief joy.* "Delight yourself in the LORD, and he will give you the desires of your heart" (Ps. 37:4). The more you contemplate him, his love, his mercy and patience, the greater will be your joy in him. You'll discover true happiness because it's his delight to give himself to you and end your endless search for satisfaction.

• *Think back to the last time you know you sinned and ask yourself*:
> * What did I think would make me happier than what I had?
> * Why do I believe that there is happiness in attaining this?
> * What makes me most afraid, angry, worried, sad? Why?
> * What is the lie that I am believing about God, myself, my happiness?
> * What do you boast about? Consider the topics of the stories you tell about yourself.

As you consider your answers to these questions, you'll begin to see your functional gods, those things that you believe will make you happy. This is a good exercise particularly when you know you're struggling with some thorny sin that you can't seem to understand or conquer. *At the heart of every one of our sanctification problems are false worship and lies about the source of real happiness.*

• *Meditate on God's goodness to you in the gospel.* Review the gospel declarations. What is he like? What has he already done for you? What does his love mean to you? What does this teach you about where real happiness resides?

• *Invite others to speak into your life and help you see your sin, particularly your unbelief and idolatry.* None of us see ourselves as we are; that's one reason why the Lord has placed us in his body, the church.

• *Prayerfully make a plan of how to respond to gospel obligations the next time you're tempted to sin.* For instance, in order to overcome my propensity to be irritated when Phil comes home earlier than expected I can:
> * Remind myself that God has bound me eternally to himself and that I don't have to fight this battle alone.
> * Remember that I've been forgiven for this sin so I'm not consigned to commit it over and over again. "No sin can be crucified in either life or heart, unless it first be pardoned in conscience, because there will be want of faith to receive the strength of Jesus, by whom alone it can be crucified. If it be not mortified in its guilt, it cannot be subdued in its power."[12]

* Remind myself that God is in control and that he is more interested in my holiness than my work for him.
* Remember that the Spirit of the living Christ is in me, and he has given me all that I need to overcome sin and be endlessly happy.
* Think soberly about my unbelief and idolatry and how Christ suffered for these sins in his body on the cross.
* Ask Phil what time he plans on getting home and then exercise self-discipline to stop writing before he arrives.
* Look for ways to demonstrate my gratitude to the Lord and to Phil; for instance, I can prepare my heart by thanking God that I accomplished all he had for me that day, even if I wasn't as productive as I would have liked; I can offer my day and all my work to him and ask him to use it for his glory; I can thank Jesus for his life of service and ask him to remind me that I'm not greater than he. If he washed feet, shouldn't I? I can put on a worship CD and then tidy up the house and begin dinner in plenty of time so that when Phil comes home, I'll be glad to see him instead of irritated by his interruption.

I Will Cleanse You from All Your Idols

I recognize that these steps might seem simplistic, but our response to gospel obligations doesn't need to be complicated, does it? Grace-motivated obedience, beginning with repentance for unbelief and turning from idols, doesn't have to be arduous because God himself is committed to our holiness. He promises:

> I will sprinkle clean water on you, and you shall be clean . . . and from all your idols I will cleanse you. And I will give you a new heart, and a new spirit I will put within you. And I will remove the heart of stone from your flesh and give you a heart of flesh. And I will put my Spirit within you, and cause you to walk in my statutes and be careful to obey my rules. . . . And you shall be my people, and I will be your God. (Ezek. 36:25–28)

Does this passage give you hope? I trust it does. We cannot remake our hearts, but he can. We cannot change our spirits, but he can place his Spirit within us. Apart from his work, we have hearts of stone, and we will walk only in our own ways. Without his sanctifying Spirit, I'll always be aggravated when I'm interrupted.

But he is changing us; he has changed us. He is cleansing us from all our idols, and he has sprinkled pure water on us and made us clean. We have a new identity. He has given us warm, living hearts of flesh and placed his Spirit in us. We can grow in grateful obedience because he has promised that we will walk in his statutes and obey his rules. He is engaged in this war we're waging; he is the Captain that has gone before us and supplied us all we need. Because he is our resurrected Lord, our struggle to put off unbelief and its fruit can be fought with boldness and confidence.

Vindicating His Holy Name

Although these are wonderful blessings, God's primary motive in our transformation isn't only our ultimate happiness, although it isn't less than that. The verses that precede the passage above tell us his goal:

> Thus says the Lord GOD: "It is not for your sake . . . but for the sake of my holy name. . . . I will vindicate the holiness of my great name. . . . And the nations will know that I am the LORD," declares the Lord GOD, "when through you I vindicate my holiness before their eyes." (Ezek. 36:22–23)

God's primary motive in our justification and sanctification is to vindicate his holiness in the sight of every nation. To accomplish this goal, he has chosen to use his Son as the primary means of advertising his perfections to a scoffing and blasphemous world. His character is so perfect, and it is so right that it be known, that he has chosen to transform hateful rebels into adoring children.

This transformation is meant to result in something very specific: *worship*. God created us to be worshipers because it is right that he be known, loved, and worshiped. This isn't because he is needy and wishes someone would tell him how special he is. No, it's because he is perfect and the worship of his perfection is holiness in action.

Because he is God and perfectly holy, everything in him revolves around him and elicits worship from all creation (Luke 19:40). When we fail in holiness, we fail because we're not centered on him, orbiting around him; we're worshiping something else. We aren't believing in his goodness; we're creating other gods to worship. But God has made us to worship him, and he is transforming us so that we will worship in the "splendor of holiness" (1 Chron. 16:29).

Although worship is God's goal, he also has great regard for our happiness. He desires our worship because our happiness is inextricably tied to our worship of him. When we think on him, rejoice in him, and praise his glorious holiness, then, and only then, will we find the happiness we're seeking. What a blessing that he has tied our happiness to his glory! As we strive to put off all the loves that captivate our hearts, may we have this picture before us: infinitely joyous worship led by the Son, empowered by the Spirit, for all eternity.

Realizing How God's Love Transforms Your Identity and Life

1) Every failure in sanctification is a failure in worship. Do you agree? Explain.

2) Read 2 Corinthians 6:16–7:1. What are the gospel declarations and obligations here?

3) Review your answers to the questions on page 137. Why is it important for us to know our unbelief and idolatries?

4) Can you explain why sanctification seems so difficult? What are the promises that encourage you as you struggle with sin?

5) Summarize in four or five sentences what you've learned from this chapter.

CHAPTER NINE

WALK IN LOVE

Therefore be imitators of God, as beloved children. And walk in love, as Christ loved us and gave himself up for us, a fragrant offering and sacrifice to God.

EPHESIANS 5:1–2

Please read the verses above and let me ask you a question or two. Without rereading it now, what do you recall about it? Are you more aware of what the verse is commanding you to do—to imitate God and to walk in love? Or are you more aware of what the verse says about who you are, a beloved child, or what Christ has done, loving you and giving himself up as an offering and sacrifice to God? Although I know that this is a contrived exercise, and that we've broached this topic before, I think that it speaks to our natural propensity to focus exclusively on our obligations. My guess is that for most of us, the focus would fall on the imperative: we're to imitate God; we're to walk in love. And although these commands are valid and binding, that's not all the verse says. No, very significantly, we're told we're God's beloved children. We aren't unwanted foster kids. No, we're his very dear children.

THE RUNAWAY BUNNIES

I have six grandchildren. Have I mentioned them before? I have a special name for them. They are my "darlings." I'll admit that I'm besotted. Recently, when the darlings have come for a visit, we've played "Runaway Bunny." In case it's been a while since you read this children's story, *Runaway Bunny*[1] is the story of a young rabbit and the imaginary game of chase he plays with his mother, as he dreams up different ways to escape her love while she blocks each of his moves. "If you run away," she replies, "I will run after you. For you are my little bunny."

We read the book together and the darlings run off down the hall, as trout in a stream, crocuses in a garden, or sailboats on the sea, and the mother bunny (me) pursues them, bringing them back to herself. They are her little bunnies. In the end, the little bunnies decide to stay home, cozily munching carrots, because their Mimi's love is so strong they can't escape it.

Let's revisit the verse this chapter opened with. In that verse God declares that you are his beloved child. You are very dear to him; he cherishes you. You are his darling, and he will faithfully block every move you try to make away from him. He loves you with the same intensity and purity of love that he has for his Son (John 17:23). Jesus is his beloved and *so are you.* The love we have for our dearest relations, the love I have for my darlings, can't be compared with the great love the Father has for us.

You Are His Darling

Think for a moment about the person you love the most in this world. Do you believe that the Father's love for you outshines this precious love to the highest degree? Our natural unbelief will always cast doubt on his love for us. It is the awareness of his love *and only this* that will equip us to wage war against sin. Until we really grasp how much he loves us, we'll never be able to imitate him. We won't come near to him if we're afraid of his judgment. We won't repent and keep pursuing godliness if we don't believe that our sin doesn't faze his love for us one bit. We won't want to be like him if we believe that his love is small, stingy, censorious, severe. And we'll never be filled with his fullness until we begin to grasp the extent of his love (Eph. 3:19). As a member of his family, you're the apple of his eye, the child he loves to bless. You're his darling.

Are you uncomfortable with this kind of language? Would you prefer to see God as transcendent, exalted, far away, untouchable? Many serious-minded believers don't have a problem seeing God as their sovereign King. I would count myself among that group, too. But God is not only transcendent and exalted; he is also immanent (Isa. 57:15), close by, as near to us as our breath. He dwells among us. His Son, Immanuel, is clothed in a body like ours, and he has brought that flesh into the throne room of heaven. We're with him right now. The Father is seated on his throne and next to him sits Jesus, clothed in flesh like ours, though glorified. His hands have touched our brothers and sisters. They cooked food, broke bread, healed lepers. He condescended to be touched, handled, seen, loved, laid in a manger, laid in a cave. Yes, he is the holy and highly exalted King of Heaven, but he is also the Good Shepherd who personally bears us in his arms all the way home.

How do we know that the Father has this kind of love for us? How can our hearts be assured before him? Simply because his dear Son loved us and gave himself up for us. He became the thank offering that we should have given. He was the sacrifice for sin that we needed. If he didn't spare his own Son, but gave his darling up for us, how can we ever doubt his love again? What a glorious love this is!

BECAUSE OF THAT, THIS . . .

In the midst of these comforting declarations, this passage challenges us with some pretty astounding obligations: we're to imitate God! How does that imperative strike you? For me, the thought of imitating God seems impossible. How could I possibly do that?

When Paul enjoins our imitation of God, he is not commanding us to be omnipresent or omniscient. There are certain attributes that God does not share with man. But there are other communicable ones that he does share with us, derived and weak though they may be. These attributes are to grow to maturity in our hearts as we consistently dwell on his love, bask in his nearness, and wage a vicious war against sin.

Paul's courage in bidding that we "imitate" God is based on one fact: we're part of his family. We're his beloved children. The family resemblance is already there. The *Holy* Spirit is indwelling. The seed *will* ultimately grow to fruition. It *will* bear fruit. These realities are our only hope, but they are not a weak "Gee, I hope so" kind of hope. They are sure, strong, settled. In the same way that each one of my darlings *will* share some of my characteristics, we *will* have some of God's. We will be able to grow in our imitation of him because we're born of him, filled with him, joined to him.

What does this family resemblance look like? Is it primarily seen in the ability to perform great miracles? Does it make us geniuses, sages, or powerful kings? On the contrary, his life within us is seen as we live a life of love, laying down our lives for others.

LIVE A LIFE OF LOVE

The family characteristic that should be most evident in us is summed up in these words: "walk in love." Every sin we commit, either by omission or commission, is a failure to love as we've been loved. Every transgression of the law finds its genesis in a stinginess of soul, a belief that we've got to protect our interests, fight for our rights, build our kingdom. These are the thoughts of orphans, not well-loved daughters and sons.

Let me demonstrate what I'm saying by examining the short list of sins that follows Ephesians 5:1–2, our key verses:

> Sexual immorality and all impurity or covetousness must not even be named among you, as is proper among saints. Let there be no filthiness nor foolish talk nor crude joking, which are out of place, but instead let there be thanksgiving. (vv. 3–5)

What is *sexual immorality*, in all its deviant forms, other than a failure to love? Sexual immorality is driven by selfishness and hatred, the desire to be satisfied, wanted, and pleased without concern for others. The sexually immoral person hasn't fully believed, rested in, and relished the immeasurable love of God in Christ, and, therefore, he will idolatrously seek to be satisfied elsewhere.[2]

What drives *covetousness* other than the thought that one hasn't been fully loved in Christ? Every time we think, "Why did she get that?" or "Why can't my life be like his?" we're failing to believe that we have a loving Father who has providentially ordered every occurrence in our lives for our ultimate happiness. What we're really saying when we envy is, "If I had a father who loved me the way his father loves him, I would have this, too!"

Every time I look at something someone else has and ask myself, *Why can't I have that?* I'm failing to love. Instead of envying the blessings they've been given, love would rejoice in their joy (Rom. 12:15), knowing that the good gifts they have, have been given them by the same Father who loves and gives good gifts to me. Love would see their blessings and celebrate the generosity of our Father.

People who are loved the way we are loved should have lives marked by extreme thanksgiving and laughter because of the mercy and generosity of our King. If we've got this kind of joy resident in our hearts, we won't have to resort to the kind of *crude joking* and *filthy talk* that marks the hearts of those looking for happiness in a world devoid of grace. Walking in his love is not so much an issue of which words may or may not be spoken, but a realization that his love is so astounding, so overwhelming, that it precludes complaining (the primary use of swear words) and crudities. This kind of speech is fueled by revenge or boastful self-love and a desire to be thought clever, edgy, funny, a man or woman of the world. Paul's imperative is that we avoid this kind of speech because it is "out of place." It's "out of place" because we no longer have to struggle to make a name for ourselves, nor hope that someone will love us, give us what we think we need, or find us clever. We're freed from this pursuit because we've been immeasurably loved by God, and our résumé has already been written; we're more sinful and flawed than we ever dared believe, but more loved and welcomed than we ever dared hope.

Put On a Life of Love

If you remember, there are both positive and negative imperatives in Scripture. In the last chapter we saw that unbelief and idolatry and all their fruit sins have to be put off. In this chapter, we'll consider the "put on" imperatives. These positives are meant to be "put on" in place of the "put offs" we discussed in the last chapter. For example, in the passage that we've been considering (Eph. 5:1–4), we find that thanksgiving should be put on in place of foolish talking and crude joking.

Considering the paradigm that unbelief and idolatry fuel all our sin, it's easy to see that thanksgiving will be absent when we don't trust God's goodness. We'll not worship him because our worship will be otherwise occupied. We'll worship false gods who deceitfully promise to give us the desired happinesses we crave.

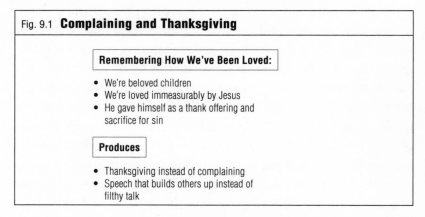

Fig. 9.1 **Complaining and Thanksgiving**

Remembering How We've Been Loved:

- We're beloved children
- We're loved immeasurably by Jesus
- He gave himself as a thank offering and sacrifice for sin

Produces

- Thanksgiving instead of complaining
- Speech that builds others up instead of filthy talk

So, then, how do we put on thanksgiving? It's not enough to merely decide that we won't complain and that we'll give thanks to God. Anyone who has tried to stop complaining on these terms will know how long that lasted. No, proper thanksgiving will be produced in the heart that:

• *knows and delights in God's love and providential care.* When we discover we've been demoted, or when our children repay all our hard work with rebellion, and we wonder whether anyone really appreciates how hard we've tried, we'll be humbled and comforted by his unwavering love. He is intensely committed to us, and intimately involved in the minutiae of our existence. Yes, being demoted feels humiliating; yes, our children's rebellion is painful. But because we've been given something that eclipses these transitory distresses, we can rejoice in every circumstance. How did Paul sing songs of praise in a Philippian dungeon? He believed in God's loving presence, and complaining, cursing, and empty joking just didn't fit with the truths of the gospel.

• *has grown in faith in his promises, believing that he will always be true to his word and that deep life change can occur.* When we face ongoing physical pain or when our struggle with sin seems interminable, we can believe that God is telling us the truth. We are truly his; the very Spirit that raised Jesus from death is now "giving life" to our mortal bodies (Rom. 8:11). We don't need to curse our pain or the medical establishment's ineptitude; we don't need to curse our failures or make jokes about our sin. We've got something better that stimulates worship within us: his promise that a day will come when all our sorrows, sins, and sicknesses will fly away and we'll be completely free. In the meantime, we can rest confidently in his sustaining grace, pray for healing and godliness, and fill our mouths with grateful thanksgiving because there's something approaching us that is more real than our present pain and failure.

• *has begun to identify the idols that animate his imagination, that cause him to become disgruntled.* For instance, the worship of approval and financial independence will engender anger when one is passed over for a much-desired promotion. Then vile speech will quickly flow from our idolatry: cursing the boss and jokes about authority and the stupidity of those who are over us will be rampant. Thanksgiving will vanish because recognition of God's gracious love and sovereignty have vanished from our consciousness. Do we need to control our speech at work? Yes. But we'll never be able to do so when our hearts are focused on our own kingdom, our supposed right to be loved, respected, rewarded; we'll never conquer our sinful speech patterns when the light of God's love isn't blazing in every aspect of our identity and life.

Our pattern of life and speech is to be completely saturated with a faith that is motivated and energized by responsive love for him. *Any obedience that isn't motivated by his great love is nothing more than penance.*

Faith Working Through Love

True gospel obedience is "faith working through love." The love that energizes grateful obedience is the heart's response to the love we've been shown (1 John 4:19). Eighteenth-century pastor William Romaine describes the joys of realizing this love: "[God] will set thee in the chariot of love, and thou shall ride on prosperously. He will oil the wheels of duty, and they shall run easy and pleasant."[3]

Paul writes that we are "through the Spirit, by faith" eagerly awaiting the hope of righteousness (Gal. 5:5). Our "gospelized" obedience must be rooted in the belief that we really do have his righteousness imputed to us. We are, right now, completely perfect in his sight. It is trust in this reality that gives us faith, hope, and courage to walk into the experiential day-by-day righteousness we long for. This is why we mustn't leave Jesus behind when we pursue godliness. Only the knowledge that we're already completely righteous before him will enable us to pursue holy living when our kids rebel, our spouses disrespect us, our employers demote us. *I can respond in love now, in this difficult time, because I've been so loved* is the only motivation powerful enough to turn self-serving penance into gospelized obedience.

Outward conformity to the law doesn't count "for anything" in the Lord's eyes (Gal. 5:6). If we decide we're going to be obedient because we think it will help us have an easier life, enable us to approve of ourselves, or earn us something from God, it's worthless. That's why Paul counted everything in which he might have boasted as rubbish—and he had plenty of religious attainments to brag about. Anything we accomplish or try to accomplish so that we can boast or reassure ourselves is destined for the garbage heap. It's vile penance, and penance is not a Christian construct because it flies in the face of the gospel. Only gospelized obedience, "faith working through love" (Gal. 5:6), is of any value. And so, if we're to put on gospel holiness, it must start in the affections, in our hearts. Every good work, if it isn't done in faith empowered by a responsive love, is simply moralistic refuse.

Right about now you might be wondering how you would know if you've fallen into patterns of penance or if your obedience is truly gospel-centered. You can tell in several ways.

• First, how do you respond when you fail? Do you spend hours in self-recrimination? Do you beat yourself up over your failures?

• How do you respond to trials? Do you think that God is punishing you for your failure to obey? Do you get angry at him for not holding up his part of the bargain?

• What about prayer? Do you love to spend time in your Father's presence or is prayer just one more duty on your checklist? Do you enjoy the fact that he enjoys spending time with you, or do you feel guilty about your failure to pray more?

• Are your emotions warm toward him, especially in worship, during the sacraments, and while hearing his Word preached? Are you hungry and thirsty for him? Do you delight in times of praise because it gives you opportunity to express the thoughts that captivate your soul, or is church attendance just one more duty to be borne out of grudging obligation?

It's in these ways that we can begin to see the underlying motives for our obedience. If your faith is energized by genuine love for him, you'll find your desire to obey and to lovingly serve others growing. Of course, our love and service will never be perfect this side of heaven, but we are being transformed, incrementally, slowly, but transformed nevertheless.

THROUGH LOVE SERVE ONE ANOTHER

Galatians 5:13–15 reads:

> For you were called to freedom, brothers. Only do not use your freedom as an opportunity for the flesh, but through love serve one another. For the whole law is fulfilled in one word: "You shall love your neighbor as yourself."

We've been granted great freedom in our Savior's love. He has done everything that we neither would nor could have done for ourselves. We're no longer under compulsion to earn righteous standing before a just Judge. But we're not to use this wonderful freedom as an opportunity to promote, satisfy, or defend our sinful desires. Instead, we're to put on a heart of love for one another. This kind of love is lived out in a life of service, a laying down of our own selfish demands and idolatry, and a pouring out of ourselves for the ones he has called us to serve. How are we to do this? We are to put on love for our neighbor. We are to love him the way we already love ourselves.[4]

Here's where gospel declarations and obligations powerfully impact us. I don't have to shove others aside, ignore them when they displease me, jostle for recognition at work, use someone for sinful pleasure, or seek to satisfy my greedy cravings. Why? I don't have to because although I've been declared unworthy, I have been given worth in him. My name has been written on his hands so it doesn't need to be written on my boss's chart. I've been brought into eternal relationship with the only One who ever really knew and loved me, and that relationship completely satisfies me.

These gospel declarations have a direct impact on the gospel obligation to curb the use of my freedoms and willingly submit myself to loving service of others that we read about above. Gospel declarations are the motivation for self-control and humble service. They will caution me about doing wrong to a neighbor, and in so doing, they will help me fulfill the law of love (Rom. 13:10).

But recognizing what the gospel has declared about us doesn't mean that we won't have to diligently, faithfully, and persistently work at a lived-out obedience. There will always be days when I'll have to say forcefully to myself, "Elyse, you don't have to fight for this; you can serve your brothers," and then I'll have to obey concretely: make dinner, speak kindly, fulfill my employer's wishes, wash the floor, offer to baby-sit, give sacrificially, let others go first. I'll work to put on love.

Without moving past all that God has done for us in Christ, we have to continually ask ourselves this question: *What is the most loving thing I can do at this moment?* Since we're frequently at a loss to know the answer, God's law can help us. Of course, we have to remember that if we're seeking to obey God's law so that we might establish our own righteousness, we're bound to fail; but this law does also help us know what the best course of action is to take. We'll never be able to obey it perfectly, but in faith and because of his love for us, we pursue it. Paul wrote:

> Owe no one anything, except to love each other, for the one who loves another has fulfilled the law. For the commandments, "You shall not commit adultery, You shall not murder, You shall not steal, You shall not covet," and any other commandment, are summed up in this word: "You shall love your neighbor as yourself." Love does no wrong to a neighbor; therefore love is the fulfilling of the law. (Rom. 13:8–10)

In every circumstance, ask yourself:

• As far as I know, am I violating any commandment by these thoughts, words, and deeds?

• Since I owe a debt of love to my Father and to my neighbor, am I paying that debt through this action, or am I ignoring it and focusing on what I selfishly want?

• Is this something I would want said to me? Am I doing to my neighbor what I want done to me?

• Am I taking for myself something that belongs to someone else—his life, his good name, his spouse, his goods, his blessings? Am I seeking instead to be extravagantly generous with my time, resources, and love?

So, then, what is the positive gospel obligation that we must pursue? Simply this: loving our neighbor the way we've been loved.

Let me reiterate that this love is lived out in very normal, run-of-the-mill ways. It's washing feet, washing dishes; it's speaking words that cleanse the soul and refraining from words that sully it; it's submitting to unrighteous authority because we submit to a righteous higher authority; it's putting aside the remote and engaging our spouse in open and attentive conversation; it's opening our lives so that others can see our sin and God's grace at work. Every one of the positive gospel imperatives in Scripture can be summed up in this: live a life of love because you've been loved. We've been taught what this love is like because he "laid down his life for us" so that "we ought to lay down our lives for the brothers" (1 John 3:16).

Be Renewed, Put Off, and Put On

What would laying your life down right now look like? I don't know. We're all in different circumstances. But there is something that he is calling each of us to do: we're to be renewed in the attitude of our mind. We're to remember the gospel, to let it renew our thoughts about who he is, who we are, what our neighbor needs. Our attitude (and the behavior that flows from it) needs to be continually informed by the gospel. We're more sinful and flawed than we ever dared believe; we're more loved and welcomed than we ever dared hope. In light of this, we're to put off all the unbelief and self-love that motivated our former identity. And then we're to live a life of loving service because we've been created in the image of a holy and righteous God who is himself love (Eph. 4:22–24). We can be faithful servants to each other because "the immortal Word took on the form of a servant,"[5] and he has gone before us, clearing the way.

Gospel-controlled Obedience

"For the love of Christ controls us, because we have concluded this: that one has died for all, therefore all have died; and he died for all, that those who live might no longer live for themselves but for him who for their sake died and was raised" (2 Cor. 5:14–15).

How are we to live this life of loving service? By letting the love of Christ control us and concluding that his death for us means that we are no longer to live for ourselves but for "him who for [our] sake died and was raised." For instance, when we're tempted to gossip about someone who has snubbed us, we're to:

• *be transformed in our attitude.* Jesus loves me and this love is so intentional, committed, and powerful that it caused him to die in my place. But he has also been resurrected, which means that right now, as I'm tempted to say something unkind about someone else, I can refuse this evil desire because he has conquered sin in my life. I don't have to live for myself any more, trying to prove my worth to others. The full measure of my worth was demonstrated on the cross. No, instead I can remember that I live for him.

• *put away the evil inclination that's calling to me right this moment.* I don't need to defend myself or prove I'm worthy of respect. Very practically speaking, I need to close my mouth while I speak to my heart: "This desire for revenge is part of my old unbelieving identity." My new identity tells me that I am not worthy of respect but have been loved and welcomed by the One who is recreating me in his image. His love is to control my words.

• *put on compassion and kindness* and treat my neighbor the way that I want to be treated. If it is loving and helpful to do so, I can speak the truth to her in love, letting her know how her actions toward me were unloving, but I can also build her up by serving her in very practical ways. I can do this because the Lord speaks to me about ways I need to change, but he never withholds his love from me while he does so.

FOLLOWING OUR SAVIOR'S FOOTSTEPS

What does living a life of gospelized obedience look like? Is it a drudgery? Is it a grinding code of conduct that punctiliously slogs through every minuscule action joylessly, meanly flogging oneself for every misstep in behavior? Is it pinching, censorious, small, dark? No, of course not. It's a life that's best understood by looking at our Savior's life.

His life was a life of love, and it was filled with service to sinful people. He joyously celebrated at parties, provided food for those who were about to turn their backs on him, hung around with thieves and prostitutes, turned water into wine. He allowed the tears of a sinful woman to wash his feet; he sat down in a crowd and spoke the truth in love. He overturned the tables (and lives) of those who sought to sell righteousness; he calmed storms and the fears of his followers; he walked up Calvary's hill. His life was marked by one conspicuous trait: love. Because he has laid down his life, because his life is coursing through us by the Spirit, we can have hope that as he was in this world, so are we (1 John 4:17). Because of his life, death, resurrection, and ascension, we can wholeheartedly pursue gospelized obedience. The sins that so easily beset us, the proud self-serving that colors all we do, can be warred against by the love that he has placed within us. War it is, yes; but it is a glorious, confident, courageous war. It's a war of love, and we already know the outcome.

Realizing How God's Love Transforms Your Identity and Life

1) Do you have hope that your life can be transformed? If so, upon what do you base that hope?

2) Define "gospelized" obedience. Define penance. Which one does your obedience most resemble? What is the key to gospelized obedience?

3) John Calvin wrote, "I am here subject to many changes, which may cause me to lose courage. But what of it? The Son of God is my Head, Who is exempt from all change. I must, then, take confidence in Him."[6] What are the "changes" that cause you to lose courage? How do the resurrection and the ascension benefit you personally?

4) Do you realize that every sin you commit is a failure to love?

Think back over your day to ascertain how this is true in your life. If you were to put on a life of love, how would this day have been different? What must be done if you're to love others tomorrow? What do you need to think on, put off, and put on?

5) Summarize in four or five sentences what you've learned from this chapter.

CHAPTER TEN

TAKE COURAGE;
YOUR SINS ARE FORGIVEN

"Take heart, my son [my daughter]; your sins are forgiven"

MATTHEW 9:2

H ere's how I've framed the thesis of this book: "In our desire
to live the Christian life, most of us have simply left Jesus
behind." I'm not saying that we've "left him behind" because we've
grown cold toward him or because we don't love him. I think we've
left him behind because we can't figure out how he applies to our
daily life. We know that the crucifixion, resurrection, and ascension
certainly ought to matter in some way; we've all heard that these
things are relevant and we do believe that they are historical facts,
but we just don't know how the realities they represent affect the
vicissitudes of the here-and-now. We have trouble connecting the
dots between Bethlehem, Calvary, the throne room of heaven, and
our daily grind. Here's how one writer summarized the importance
of making these connections: *"All progress in the Christian life
depends upon a recapitulation of the original terms of one's acceptance with God."*[1] In other words, every forward step depends upon
summing up the main points of the gospel and then living them out
in our lives. Over and over again, we've got to take ourselves back
to the incarnation, the crucifixion, the resurrection, and the ascension or we won't make much real progress in the Christian life.

Remember, real progress in the Christian life is not gauged
by our knowledge of Scripture, our church attendance, time in

prayer, or even our witnessing (although it isn't less than these things). Maturity in the Christian life is measured by only one test: how much closer to his character have we become? The result of the Spirit's work is not more and more activity. No, the results of his work are seen in our quality of life; they are "love, joy, peace, patience, kindness, goodness, faithfulness, gentleness, self-control" (Gal. 5:22–23). It is life like his.

In order to grow in Christlikeness, we've got to intentionally apply the gospel to everything we are and everything we long to do. We're not to sever our obedience from his perfect sinlessness nor disconnect our mortal life from his resurrected life. We've got to understand ourselves in the light of our new identity, seeing ourselves as we truly are: sinful and flawed, loved and welcomed. Only these gospel realities have enough power to engender faith, kill idolatry, produce character change, and motivate faithful obedience.

YOUR SINS ARE FORGIVEN

How does the statement "your sins are forgiven" strike you? Is it a given? *Oh yes, I'm saved. My sins are forgiven.* Yes, it's comforting, but is it riveting? Has it slid out to the fringes of a creed you believe in but aren't gripped by? Is it basically a statement about something that should be significant but doesn't seem to have much transforming power?

In Matthew's Gospel we read of a paralytic who was brought to Jesus by his friends. Perhaps they were family members or just men who had known him before he was paralyzed. We don't know who they were, but we can surmise what they wanted. What were they hoping for? Healing, of course. This invalid and his friends were hoping that Jesus would enable him to do what he wanted to do: walk, live a normal life. But Jesus had a different perspective on this man's true need. Instead of saying initially, "Be healed. Rise and walk," he said, "Take heart, my son; your sins are forgiven" (Matt. 9:2).

Jesus saw that the paralytic had a more pressing need than

his obvious, physical one. He wasn't simply a cripple in need of a healthy spinal cord. No, he was a coward in need of faith, an orphan in need of a father, a sinner in need of a Savior. And so Jesus said to him, "Take heart, my son; your sins are forgiven." By these eight words, Jesus transformed his identity and life.

Jesus' first words to him were "take heart." In saying this he wasn't merely encouraging him to look on the sunny side. No, he was telling him to have courage, to be confident, to shun the fear that gripped his heart. In several other instances where Jesus used this phrase, he followed it with "be not afraid."[2] This man was looking for healing, and I'm sure he was fearful—fearful that he would be disappointed, that he would be shunned, that his hopes would again be dashed. The Lord looked right into his heart, and he told the man what he needed to hear. Not, "you're healed," but "don't be afraid."

The Lord then calls him "my son." These are words of relationship, words spoken to assure the hearer that the Lord saw him as a person, a person he knew. To Jesus he wasn't just a stranger, an outsider begging for a favor from someone who had no concern for him. No, he was God's son even though he didn't yet know it.

Perhaps, after hearing those four words, the man thought that his healing was assured. But instead, Jesus said something that must have astounded, confused, and disappointed him all at the same time. He said, "Your sins are forgiven." Can you imagine what those words meant to this poor man who was not only crippled but blind to his own spiritual need? Can you imagine what flashed through his mind? *My sins forgiven? But I need healing!* And in that way, perhaps we're more like him than we know. We come to Jesus expecting him to help us lose weight or make us successful businessmen or send us a spouse or make others treat us the way we want to be treated. But Jesus has something different to say to us, something far more important. Jesus says to us, "Have faith in me. I love you and have made you my own. I've suffered for your sin and you're completely forgiven."

The Lord who loved him perfectly and understood him completely knew his true need. Of course, the Lord went on to heal him, primarily to prove his authority to forgive sin as God's Son, but there was other, more pressing business to be done first. The man needed assurance that faith in Christ wouldn't be disappointed. And above all else, he needed to know that his sins were forgiven. Did he need healing? Yes, of course. But he needed something far more important—and so do we. *Rather than the truths of forgiveness and faith being ancillary in our lives, everything else needs to be ancillary to them.* Nothing—not your position at work, not your children's successes, not your physical attractiveness, *nothing*—is more important than this.

In order to help you make connections between the wonderful truths we've been studying (the indicatives) and your daily lives, I'm going to sketch four situations[3] for you and help you see how the gospel is not only pertinent but necessary for growth in Christlikeness.

I Can't Let Myself Gain Weight!

Jane is a seventeen-year-old high school senior who has struggled with habits of self-starvation, self-induced vomiting, and over-exercise for three years. She is a believer and recognizes that her troubling behavior is sinful and is damaging her health. She's absolutely terrified by the thought that she might become fat, but at the same time she's terrified by what might happen if she doesn't change. She's tried to stop the behavior but hasn't had much success. Now the question is, how does the gospel speak to Jane and her sin?

The Incarnation

The fact that God became man tells her that he knows what it's like to be human, to be encased in flesh. He isn't a disembodied spirit; he knows what it feels like to eat food, to be tired. Having a body isn't an evil; it's a good because God has forever taken one to himself. Bethlehem also tells her of a love so infinite that Jesus was willing to confine his human nature to a body of flesh so that he might bring her to himself as his bride.

His Sinless Life

Because Christ lived perfectly, obeying every law in her place, Jane doesn't have to strive for perfection on her own. She can stop her frantic fig-leaf construction because he's already clothed her with "robes of righteousness."

The Crucifixion

Even though Jane is filled with unbelief and idolatry and all the resultant sins that flow from them, Christ already bore (and will continue to bear) every one of those sins in her place. Her sin does, indeed, deserve God's wrath, but his wrath has been fully expended on his Son. She's completely forgiven for all her self-focus and self-love and for all her fear, dishonesty, harsh words, comparing, vanity, and selfishness.

The Resurrection

Because Jesus was raised from the dead, she can be assured of two things: first, his sacrifice was accepted by God, and he has forgiven her. Secondly, the power of the sins of unbelief, self-love, and self-worship has truly been broken in her life. She can have faith to continue to do battle against these sins because Jesus has gone before her and assured her of her ultimate glorification. Even though these sins may feel more powerful than her faith, she can assure herself of the truth that she's now living a new life, empowered by the resurrected Son of God.

The Ascension

Because Jesus is now seated at the right hand of the Father, still enfleshed though glorified, her body isn't loathsome to the Father. In fact, he loves her and will eventually bring her, body and soul, into his presence. Because she is already beautiful to him, she can begin to enjoy her body rather than see it as her enemy or her identity. In addition, her Savior is speaking to the Father on her behalf, praying for her, sending his Spirit to her, granting her grace and sustaining faith.

In light of all these wonderful gospel declarations, she can approach the imperatives in faith and seek to put on ordinary, grateful obedience. The humility that automatically flows out of an intentional embracing of the gospel will tell her what she needs to know: she is, indeed, sinful and flawed, but her sin doesn't begin and end with her eating habits. She's an idolater, a self-worshiper, working out her own righteousness, building her own kingdom, desiring the worship of others.

But that's not all the gospel says about her. It also says that she's loved and welcomed. These sins are already fully paid for, and Jesus has already lived perfectly in her place. He sought only his Father's approval, and he had it; he demonstrated true inward and outward righteousness; he gave his body for her body and soul, and he built the Father's kingdom for his glory. All these perfections are hers in him.

Then, in light of all these truths, she must valiantly pursue holiness by identifying the lies she's always believed: "I would be worthless if I were fat; my real worth is based on whether I can approve of myself." She's got to be renewed in her mind, realizing that her outer man is decaying, but her inner man is being renewed day by day. She's got to see that Jesus Christ has declared her worth in his love; because he loves her she doesn't have to strive to attain the love and respect of others. Next, she's got to put off the behaviors that flow from these lies: starving herself, weighing herself incessantly, gluttonous eating, and over-exercising. At the same time, she's got to put on godliness: humbly confessing her sins to other sisters and asking for help and focusing her life on the service of others. What does she need to hear? "Take courage, Jane. You're already my daughter. Your sins are forgiven."

THIS IS MY TIME!

Success is written everywhere on George's countenance. He's got a beautiful multimillion-dollar home in one of the most coveted neighborhoods in the world. He's at the top of his game, head of marketing for the computer software company he's been with for decades. His kids are grown and doing well; his wife is gracious and loving. Sure, he is a Christian, and his Christianity is important to him, but his wife would say that his business is more important than anything else. And although now is the time when he should be able to relax a bit and enjoy the fruit of his labor, his company is facing the possibility of losing a lawsuit, and if it does, the company will file bankruptcy. Everything he has worked for is about to go up in smoke, and what's worse, some of the stockholders are intimating that the lawsuit was due to his negligence. He has begun to drink excessively, and he wakes up every night in a panic. He feels that he can't relax for one moment because if he does, it might "all slip away." He is irritable, confused, and wondering what he did to deserve this. He wonders how all his hard work could possibly eventuate in his being a failure. He wonders why God isn't protecting his position. How will the gospel help him?

The Incarnation

The humiliation that is part and parcel of the incarnation is something George has unwittingly avoided his whole life. Christ's self-emptying is completely antithetical to what he thinks God wants for him. Although his wife has suffered from his absence for years, he would counter by saying that he has provided a nice living for her and their children. He needs to see how the incarnation means *self-sacrificing relationship*, not merely provision of material needs. Jesus Christ was not too busy in heaven to be stripped and to embrace the burden of fellowship with George.

His Sinless Life

The wonderful news for George is that Jesus Christ lived the life George should have been living all along. Jesus left his celestial palace and eschewed self-promotion, continually seeking only the glory of his Father (John 5:41–44). He was born in a stable. He worked at menial tasks with his hands: shaping wood, catching fish. He had no place to lay his head and was despised by the wealthy. He worked for true riches so that George's spiritual bankruptcy would never be felt by him, and he laid down his life for his bride.

The Crucifixion

George has been fighting his whole life to prove that he is a success, all the while never seeing the cross for what it was: an indictment and conviction of his abject failure. The things he should have concentrated on he has ignored, but his Savior has borne the full wrath of the Father in George's place. Every unkind word, every drop of alcohol meant to anesthetize the soul, every time he ignored his wife's pleas for fellowship, was placed upon his suffering Savior. George needs to understand that he is, indeed, an utter failure, but his failure isn't simply that he might lose his material wealth; he has failed to love God or his neighbor. But Jesus Christ groaned in agony in his place.

The Resurrection

Although George might feel hopeless, the resurrection tells him about hope. His hope must not be that life will continue as it always has and that his job will be protected. No, his hope must be that although suffering may continue for a season, joy is assured in the morning. His Savior has completed all the work that needed to be done and then he offered himself in ignominious suffering, but the story doesn't end there. Jesus Christ conquered death, and now, because Christ lives, George's greatest fears can be put to rest. He doesn't need to prove his worth anymore, and he also doesn't need to live in fear and despair. By the power of the Spirit, he can change; he can become the man God is calling him to be.

The Ascension

Christ's victorious rule brings great hope and comfort to George. His life and career are not at the mercy of stockholders or judges, but are instead being watched over by a Man who understands him and has the ear of the King.

In light of all this truth, George needs to repent of his self-centered ambition and his love of success. He also needs to repent for withholding fellowship from the one person for whom he is particularly to lay down his life, his wife. The lie he has always believed, "In order to be happy I must be successful," must be replaced with the truth: "I am completely sinful and flawed, but I am also loved and welcomed." He needs to love relationships as he once loved success.

He needs to confess his sins to a group of friends who will come alongside him, encouraging him, praying for him, confronting him, when he begins to give in again to habits of self-promotion. He needs to refrain from any form of self-indulgence and instead ask the Lord to open his eyes to his true need. What does he need to hear? "Take courage, George, my son. Your sins are forgiven."

MARY'S LIFE IN THE CAVE

From all outward appearances, Mary really does have a pretty good life. That's why everyone is astounded when they discover she hasn't been out of bed in a week and is talking about suicide. Mary's husband is a diligent provider, and although they struggle financially, he does try to be a good husband and father. Her children, aged seven and nine, are normal kids. Recently the heater in their house broke and her car is on its last leg, so her husband is picking up extra hours at work to try to get everything fixed. So, why is Mary so unhappy? She is unhappy because she always believed that if she served God, he would provide a nice home for her so that she could prove to her mother and sisters that she isn't the loser she's always been accused of being.

The Incarnation

Like George, Mary needs to see how Jesus eschewed riches for the sake of others. Although she would say that she doesn't want to be "rich," the truth is that her love of money is filling her whole soul with darkness (Matt. 6:19–24). Her Savior became poor so that she might become a partaker of true riches, and his withholding of the comforts of life from her is a function of this same self-emptying love. Even though he had always been loved and worshiped in heaven, his life on earth was marked by betrayal, misunderstanding, and false accusation. One day they worshiped him and threw palm branches before him. The next day they threw insults at him and cried, "Crucify, crucify!" Whether her family approves of her or not, her Savior took on the form of a lowly servant for her sake and because of this, she can embrace her role as servant and fight the desire to be worshiped.

His Sinless Life

Her Redeemer's life was marked by humble obedience, performed with the pure motive of bringing glory to his Father. He didn't think he would be shielded from suffering because of his obedience; in fact the opposite was true. The anger and self-pity that has fueled Mary's retreat into suicidal speech is driven by her belief that she has worked hard enough so that she deserves better than what she's getting. Of course, she's completely deceived about what she's earned, but the wonderful news is that even so, she's got the perfect record of another.

The Crucifixion

While on the cross, Jesus Christ bore the just wrath Mary deserves for living life for any purpose other than the glory of God. He bore the crushing for her proud belief that she could be good enough to earn anything from God. He felt the bruising that should have been hers because she thought that God was unjust and unkind. He was forsaken by his Father because she had forsaken her Savior and loved and worshiped mammon.

The Resurrection

Mary can face the day before her, whether it is filled with the disapproval of her family or the breakdown of her washer. She can face these things because she's got a Savior who suffered in her place, purchasing her acceptance with God, and she's also been assured of his adoption, an adoption into a family whose members all have the same record: beloved sinner. She also has a guarantee of marrying up: she's betrothed to the risen Lord, and this betrothal is the most important factor about who she is.

The Ascension

Her heavenly fiancé is watching closely over her life, providing as the loving Husband he is for everything she truly needs. He is calling her to arise and come to him in faith, to believe that his words about her are more important than her mother's, to trust herself into his providential care.

Mary needs to repent of her unbelief and idolatry. She's failed to believe that God is really good and has her best interests at heart. She has also failed to believe that he can satisfy her. She hasn't seen the depth of her idolatry, her love of her family's approval, her belief that she can be good enough to "earn" anything besides hell. She needs to repent of her "splendid vices," those good works she's done to try to ingratiate herself to God.

In light of all this, Mary needs to confess her sins to others and ask for help and accountability. When she's tempted to give herself over to self-pity, she needs to seek out ways to love others and fulfill her responsibilities as best she can—for God's glory. When she's tempted to wonder what he has done for her today, she needs to remember the gospel, repent of her self-righteousness and covetousness, and express gratitude for her husband's willingness to work.

She needs to make a list of the responsibilities she needs to complete every day, offer her work to the Lord, and then work.

THE LURE OF THE LURID

Mike is a good-looking, upwardly mobile, married Christian man with a beautiful Christian wife and darling twin daughters. He is not wealthy, but he is diligent, and he is working hard to make a home for his family. Mike's got a secret though. He has been visiting porn sites on the Internet for some time, and now he's developed an attraction to the new receptionist in the office. He loves his wife and daughters, but this other woman is flirtatious and obviously interested in him. One little visit with her over coffee wouldn't be that big of a deal would it? What does Mike need to remember about the gospel?

The Incarnation

Mike is in desperate need of a reminder about the incarnation. His Savior took on flesh, put aside his rightful pleasures, and embraced the form of a servant out of love for Mike's soul. Every relationship his Redeemer had with a woman was always aimed at her best interest. Jesus loved women and didn't use them for his own selfish gain. In his manhood, Jesus was no sissy. He wasn't immune to a righteous desire to be one with another; he knew that aloneness was not good. But he denied himself instant gratification so that his wedding day with his bride would be fully joyous and blessedly pure.

The Sinless Life

Even though Mike isn't loving his female neighbors like he loves himself, he's got a Savior who has done that in his place. When Jesus taught that the whole law was summed up in these two laws: "love God and love your neighbor as yourself," he himself was subject to that law.

The Crucifixion

When on the cross, Mike's Redeemer suffered for all the adultery Mike has already committed in his heart. Although following through on his plan for "coffee" with this other woman would bring great suffering to those closest to him, Mike has already caused his Savior agony for his wandering lusts. Even so, Jesus Christ bore every ounce of wrath his Father had for all Mike's sins, and Mike stands fully justified before him.

The Resurrection

The power of Mike's enslavement to pornography and temptation to adultery was broken when Jesus Christ died for his sin and then was raised by the Spirit of the Father. Mike is completely new. He's got a new identity. He is a beloved adopted son with more gifts than he will ever be able to number. He has been loved by the Father and completely welcomed into his family. He doesn't have to idolize being desired by other women anymore, because he has been desired and captured by his Savior's holy love.

The Ascension

Jesus stands in heaven now, the God-Man. He isn't a high priest who is insensible to the temptations of Mike's manhood, but one who has instead walked through all these temptations without sin. And now he calls Mike to "with confidence draw near to the throne of grace, that [he] may receive mercy and find grace to help in time of need" (Heb. 4:16). Mike can be assured of Jesus' help because Jesus has promised to save him to the uttermost and cleared away every obstacle that might have thwarted his ultimate journey home.

In light of all these truths, Mike needs to repent of his hatred of women and his desire to use them for his own self-aggrandizement. He needs to learn that women are co-equal with him before God, and that when he views pornography, entertains thoughts of a tryst with another woman, or lies to his wife, he is not loving his neighbor as he loves himself. He is, in fact, hating them and endangering their souls for his own selfish short-lived pleasures.

He needs to confess his sin to a group of men who will hold him accountable and help him employ whatever means necessary to obstruct his pornography use. He needs to confess his sins to his wife, and he must ask her to pray for him and then humble himself as she works through the breach of trust that he has occasioned. If necessary, he needs to ask to be reassigned or he needs to look for a different job in order to flee the lust that he has allowed to grow. He needs to think about the purity and protection of his daughters and then seek to be the kind of father to them that he needs to be.

Of course, there is so much more to say about each of these problems. This section isn't meant to tell you everything that should be said or done but, rather, is meant to give you an introduction to what applying the gospel to everyday life might look like.

Let This Mind Be in You

Everything that we've just talked about in these simulated vignettes is illustrated in Philippians 2, where we find gospel declarations and gospel obligations and the motive behind gospelized obedience.

> Do nothing from rivalry or conceit, but in humility count others more significant than yourselves. Let each of you look not only to his own interests, but also to the interests of others. Have this mind among yourselves, which is yours in Christ Jesus, who, though he was in the form of God, did not count equality with God a thing to be grasped, but made himself nothing, taking the form of a servant, being born in the likeness of men. And being found in human form, he humbled himself by becoming obedient to the point of death, even death on a cross. Therefore God has highly exalted him and bestowed on him the name that is above every name, so that at the name of Jesus every knee should bow, in heaven and on earth and under the earth, and every tongue confess that Jesus Christ is Lord, to the glory of God the Father. (Phil. 2:3–11)

In light of the gospel, Jane, George, Mary, and Mike all need to apply this passage to themselves. Jane's vain self-interest must be slain by Christ's gracious self-emptying. George's grasping ambition must be transformed into humble service, and the love of money and status transformed into the love of a Savior who "though he was rich, yet for [his] sake he became poor" (2 Cor. 8:9). Mary's self-pity must be swallowed up in the joy of a glorified Savior who has provided all she needs at great cost to his own person and who will command all worship. Mike's lustful self-interest must be drowned in the interests of his wife and daughters, as Christ's coexistence with God was overwhelmed by Mike's need.

TAKE COURAGE; YOUR SINS ARE FORGIVEN

So now, before you focus on the ways you need to change, spend a good long time looking at the gospel. You've got a new identity: you're God's adopted son. You've got a perfect record; you don't have to try to prove anything about yourself or seek to assure yourself any longer. Christ's perfect righteousness is yours. Because of this, you've got never-ending relationship with the Joy of the Whole Earth; this relationship will never end because you've been made a partaker of his life, and you're completely redeemed and reconciled with him. All this has been given to you by faith, which was also given to you.

In light of all these blessings, then, let me encourage you to pursue all the gospel obligations that you've always tried to pursue, but now with a different motive and energy. You're being transformed because of his great love, and that's all that matters about you. Take courage, daughter or son; your sins are forgiven.

REALIZING HOW GOD'S LOVE TRANSFORMS YOUR IDENTITY AND LIFE

1) Apply the gospel to your life. What are the declarations God has made about you? What are the imperatives that you now must pursue?

2) Define the gospel. Hint: "I am more sinful and flawed than I ever . . ."

3) Write out Philippians 2:3–11. What would having this attitude look like in your life? How does your heart militate against it?

4) What does it mean to you that Jesus Christ said, "Take courage. Your sins are forgiven"?

5) Summarize in four or five sentences what you've learned from this chapter.

CHAPTER ELEVEN

GOSPEL-CENTERED RELATIONSHIPS

Then the LORD God said, "It is not good that the man should be alone."

GENESIS 2:18

A number of years ago, my husband and I had the wonderful opportunity to vacation in Europe. In about three and a half weeks we visited thirteen different nations. When we'd enter a country, we'd get our passports stamped, exchange currencies, learn a few key phrases, and then off we'd go to visit the natives. We'd wander through outdoor markets, peruse museums, sample the cuisine. We'd exchange a few niceties with the locals, sit on the steps of cathedrals, watch the life of the town go by, take a picture or two, and purchase a little something to remind us of our time there, and then we were off. We had a wonderful vacation. Our hearts weren't changed in any significant ways by our little visits, but then they weren't meant to be. We were tourists.

THE TOURIST-DRIVEN CHURCH

It seems to me that what I've just described is very close to many people's understanding of the congregational life of the local church. On any given Sunday, or better yet, Saturday night, many tourists can be found in church. They pop in for forty-five minutes or an hour, sing a chorus or two, exchange niceties with the locals: "Hi! How are you?" "Fine! How are you?" "Fine! Nice fellowshiping with you!" They sample some of the local cuisine, they might purchase a book or CD to remind them of their visit, and then they race to their cars to get to their favorite restaurant before the rush or home before the game. For many people, church is simply a place to go once a week. It is about being a tourist, and our land is filled with tourist-friendly churches. *Pop in, pop out, do your religious thing, catch ya later!*

THE PROGRAM-DRIVEN CHURCH

I know that most of my readers don't think of themselves as tourists in church. For many of us, the church is the focal point of our lives. Let me see if I can describe what our common experience is like: our main meeting, where the real action is, is on Sunday morning. We gather together, we sing, we're led in congregational prayer, we greet one another, we contribute money, we listen to announcements, we hear a sermon, we sing a song, we leave. If we're really committed, we attend Sunday school. We might also attend a Sunday evening service or a midweek Bible study. For the really committed Christian, our congregational life isn't so much spent as tourists racing through a country, shopping, sampling cuisine; no, it's spent as if we are students attending classes meant to teach us about life in a country without our ever living with the people of that country.

Please don't assume from this that I'm saying that I believe it's wrong to gather together on Sundays or seek to learn from studying the Bible together. I'm not saying that at all. I'm fully and joyously committed to our church's corporate gatherings. I believe we've been commanded to meet together to be instructed, to offer worship, to use our gifts in service, and to receive grace through the sacraments. I'm not saying we shouldn't gather like this, but I am saying that we're missing a significant portion of what normal Christian life is all about. Normal Christian life is all about relationships: relationships with Christ, and through him with one another.

THE CHURCH AS FAMILY

The New Testament church, in part because of the great persecution she faced and in part because of the familial nature of the culture, was a tightly knit *family in relationship*. They thought of themselves as family, as fathers and mothers, brothers and sisters, living life together. In fact, the relationships they had with their Christian brothers and sisters were frequently more meaningful and binding than the ones they had with their biological families. They had a new identity, an identity defined by a common adoption. They frequently lived together or sacrificially shared their material goods, because so many had been cut off from jobs, homes, inheritances. Although it was extremely difficult for them, they knew that this was the way congregational life was to be lived out: in close, deep, biblical relationship. It's also the way that our congregational life is meant to be lived today, even though most of us aren't suffering persecution in the ways they were. John Piper declared:

> For most Christians corporate church life is a Sunday morning worship service and that's all. A smaller percentage add to that a class of some kind, perhaps Sunday morning or Wednesday evening in which there is very little interpersonal ministry. Now don't misunderstand me, I believe in the tremendous value of corporate worship and I believe that solid teaching times are usually crucial for depth and strength. But you simply can't read the New Testament in search of what church life is supposed to be like and come away thinking that worship services and classes are the sum total of what church was supposed to be.[1]

THE NATURE OF YOUR GOD

Congregational church life is not just "services and classes." It is not less than that, but it is vastly more. It is communal relationship. The primary relationship every Christian has is with our Father and with his Son. Every other relationship is simply a reflection of this one great love. Without this relationship, a thousand other relationships don't amount to anything. This is the ultimate point of our existence: to know God and Jesus Christ his Son (1 John 5:19–20). Every other relationship we have is based on this one (1 John 1:7). The only way that we are enabled to love is because we've been loved. We can be open and transparent only because we recognize that we're all of us sinful and flawed, yet loved. We don't need to pretend anymore. We're all so loved and welcomed that we don't need to fight for popularity, dominate our friends, or exclude others; we can love and welcome them. We can love because we've been loved.

We're called to be people in relationship because our God is a God in relationship. He is *three* persons in *one*. Our Savior is two natures in one. Ontologically, that is, in his very being, God is a community in relationship, and thereby he declares communal relationship not only nice but good and necessary.

Just think: the very first negative assessment made at the beginning of the world was, "It is not good that the man should be alone" (Gen. 2:18). Aloneness is not good; in fact it is evil. We know this because our God is perfect, and he perfectly discerns and displays what is good and what is not good. Intentional aloneness is not good; relationship with him and with others is.[2]

Not only does he have unbridled, unceasing community within himself, he also seeks community and family outside of himself, with us. He died to purchase a bride. He calls us his children. He invites us to know him and to be known by him (1 Cor. 13:12). He reveals himself to us (1 Cor. 2:10) and he searches our inmost beings (Rev. 2:23). He joins us to himself in eternal union, without asking us to lose our individuality. Just as he doesn't lose his individuality even though he is three persons in unity, so we don't lose ours, though we are spiritually joined to him (1 Cor. 6:17). He still calls us by name.

The Lord, in whose image we're made and being remade, is intensely committed to develop and sustain relationships within his person and with us, his children. Every action of humility and self-offering he makes is to this one end: to further relationships. Growth in self-offering, loving, transparent, committed relationship is truly what it means to grow into his likeness.

We know that the Father is passionate about relationships because his Son is passionate about them. While he walked on earth, he was part of a family, with a mother, an earthly father, sisters, and brothers. He didn't need a family in order to survive, did he? The One who multiplied loaves and fishes had close friends whose homes he frequented for meals. He was found among the crowds, the seventy, the twelve, the three (Peter, James, and John) and the one (John). Jesus had a close circle of friends, and he had a best friend. This was normal and good and part of what it meant for him to live out his nature as the Son of God.

When sin entered the garden, the primary consequence was a deep rupture in relationships. Adam and Eve were estranged from each other, fearing and blaming one another. They sewed together fig leaves to hide their nakedness. They hid from God, and fellowship with him terrified them. They constructed new identities: the angry, blame-shifting husband and the deceived, bitter wife. They were banished from the garden and excluded from open relationship with their Father. They would forever think of themselves as alienated, as orphans. Paradise was lost.

OUR RELATIONSHIP LIVED OUT WITH OTHERS

Through our relationship with him and our relationships with other believers, God is in the process of restoring his image in us. He is making us like himself. He does this by his Spirit as his grace and Word is applied to our lives through the incarnational ministry of believers one-to-another. God uses means to inform and transform us, and the primary means that he uses to do this are relationships in the local church.

As I've traveled around the country, speaking at good Bible-believing churches, I've discovered that the kind of biblical relationship to which I think the New Testament calls us is almost nonexistent. For example, I recently spoke at a conference that was well attended by women who were serious about their faith. They weren't "playing church," and they wouldn't have thought of themselves as tourists. But when I asked for a show of hands of those who were in a biblical relationship with others to whom they regularly confessed sin, expected accountability, and regularly confronted the sins of those same others, only a smattering of hands went up. That's not to say these dear sisters weren't eager to follow the Lord. It was just that this kind of relationship, this depth of biblical fellowship, was way beyond their normal practice.

The kind of fellowship I'm enjoining flies right in the face of our American individualism and desire for privacy. We don't want anyone poking around in our affairs, and we certainly don't want to be accused of poking about in anyone else's. *This idolatry of privacy and individualism is one of the greatest detriments to sanctification in the church today.* God has placed us in a family because we don't grow very well on our own. It's still not good to be alone. We need the encouragement, correction, and loving involvement of others who are willing to risk everything for the sake of the beauty of his bride.

He Gave Himself for Her

I am not now, after all this time, changing the focus of this book. In speaking about appropriate church relationships, I'm not forgetting Jesus. Instead, the whole point of what I'm encouraging you to be involved in has its genesis, expectation, and motivation in him. Paul wrote:

> Rather, speaking the truth in love, we are to grow up in every way into him who is the head, into Christ, from whom the whole body, joined and held together by every joint with which it is equipped, when each part is working properly, makes the body grow so that it builds itself up in love. (Eph. 4:15–16)

Jesus is the one we are to "grow up in every way into." His character fleshed out in our lives is his goal. He is the One who powerfully holds the whole body together and who causes it to grow strong so that it builds itself up in love. This growing together into his nature would be impossible without his transforming power and, apart from his will, we would never desire it. It is for his pleasure that we work to beautify and adorn his bride. This intentional communal life is for him, through him, and to him.

But how does this growth happen? How are we built up in love? We grow and are built up when the truth is consistently, courageously, and lovingly spoken to us by others. This is not merely the truth of one isolated or disconnected doctrine, but rather how that doctrine specifically relates to, impacts, and transforms the way that we live on a daily basis. We grow when each part is "working properly" in tandem with every other one, using the gifts of wisdom, insight, encouragement, confrontation, comfort, or prayer that he has supplied by his Spirit. Maturity in Christ does not occur because we attend Bible studies. Maturity in Christ occurs when, by the Spirit and in God's grace, our brothers and sisters take biblical truth and apply it lovingly, patiently, boldly to our hearts. In the same way that I've encouraged you to remember the Lord in your pursuit of godliness, I'm now encouraging you to see that the primary way he'll minister truth to you is through deep and transparent relationship with others.

In a well-known passage about marriage we can discover some significant truth about biblical fellowship. Here's the passage:

> Husbands, love your wives, as Christ loved the church and gave himself up for her, that he might sanctify her, having cleansed her by the washing of water with the word, so that he might present the church to himself in splendor, without spot or wrinkle or any such thing, that she might be holy and without blemish. (Eph. 5:25–27)

In this passage, we see the love our Savior has for us. He loves us, his bride, the church. He gave himself up for us so that we might be sanctified and cleansed. He washes his bride with his Word for the ultimate pleasure of presenting her to himself, in splendor, purity, and holiness. The passage continues, "In the same way husbands should love their wives." Although this is primarily a passage for husbands, it does teach us a broader truth: *Jesus uses sinful human beings to prepare his bride.* He uses them to cleanse her, to wash her with the Word, to make her ready for her wedding day. This cleansing and preparation flows from his love and is motivated by his desire for her but is carried out *primarily through ordinary means*: husbands loving wives, wives ministering to husbands, brothers and sisters helping one another through gospelized fellowship.

GOSPELIZED FELLOWSHIP

On the night that our Savior was betrayed, he did something astonishing. Here's the narrative from John 13:

> Jesus . . . rose from supper. He laid aside his outer garments, and taking a towel, tied it around his waist. Then he poured water into a basin and began to wash the disciples' feet and to wipe them with the towel that was wrapped around him. He came to Simon Peter, who said to him, "Lord, do you wash my feet?" Jesus answered him, "What I am doing you do not understand now, but afterward you will understand." Peter said to him, "You shall never wash my feet." Jesus answered him, "If I do not wash you, you have no share with me." Simon Peter said to him, "Lord, not my feet only but also my hands and my head!" Jesus said to him, "The one who has bathed does not need to wash, except for his feet, but is completely clean." . . . When he had washed their feet and put on his outer garments and resumed his place, he said to them, "Do you understand what I have done to you? You call me Teacher and Lord, and you are right, for so I am. If I then, your Lord and Teacher, have washed your feet, you also ought to wash one another's feet. For I have given you an example, that you also should do just as I have done to you. (John 13:3–10, 12–15)

Think of it. The high King of heaven condescended to bow before the dirty feet of his friends and wash them. This act of humiliation stands forever as an example of humble love and service. Now, let me ask: Do you think that Jesus was simply instituting another ritual for his followers in washing their feet and telling them to follow his example? Although there probably isn't anything wrong in having an actual "foot washing" service, I think we're missing the point if we limit our imitation of him to a simple ceremony once every six months or so.

This is the point of what I believe Jesus is teaching us. He has already spiritually cleansed each of his children from their sin. We are "completely clean," as he said. But why then, if we're already "completely clean," would he encourage us to follow his example and wash each other's feet? We need to wash one another because as each of us traverses through this world, we are immersed in and subsequently sullied by every kind of sin, unbelief, and idolatry. Sometimes that filth finds a little crevice (or large gaping wound) to incubate in, and if we're not careful, it can become infected before we know it.

You know, our feet are one of those places that, unless we're very limber or under the age of five, we can't really see very well. Not long ago I was taking an evening stroll with a friend on the beach. We were barefoot, and I couldn't clearly see where I was walking. At some point I stepped on something sharp that felt like a bee sting, and by the time I got back to my car it was itchy and painful. Then, try as I might, I just couldn't get a good glimpse of it. Finally, when I returned home, I needed to have Phil take a look. I needed his eyes to help me see what turned out to be a little thorn that I was apparently allergic to. I don't think it's inconsequential that Jesus framed this discussion around our feet. We need to wash one another, to carefully probe, cleanse, disinfect, and heal each other, and this isn't something we can see clearly enough to do on our own. We need the eyes and hands of others.

What's really delightful about all this is that not only do we help others when we "wash their feet," but our own souls are helped as well. If nothing else, our souls are humbled as we experience Christ's humility, but we are also cleansed in the process. As a biblical counselor, I can personally testify to the hundreds of times I've been encouraged, cleansed, convicted, and blessed when I helped someone else with their sin.

What I'm suggesting is that you look at the relationships you have with other believers in a new way. I'm hoping that you have begun to see yourself as an instrument that your Savior will use in your friends' lives, and that you'll begin to look for opportunities in which a friend can help you get at that painful, itchy thorn you just can't see. Because I'm assuming that this might be new in your experience, I'm going to give you some practical suggestions about how to begin to live out gospelized fellowship.

Living Out Gospelized Fellowship

First of all, let me encourage you to start small. Our Savior had twelve disciples, but he also had three close friends and one best friend. Start there. Start with two or three others who are willing to get together for biblical fellowship once a week or so. My guess is that you probably already do get together with your friends fairly frequently. So why not turn this visit, at least part of it, into a time of true biblical fellowship? If you're very busy with small children or long commutes, then why not commit to talking on the phone at least once a week, with a commitment to visit in person for a couple of hours once a month?

It's my opinion that this kind of biblical fellowship happens best in small groups that meet regularly during the month. My husband, Phil, and I presently facilitate a small group as part of our church's communal life where we are primarily focused on speaking into each other's lives through words of encouragement, correction, accountability, and the open confession of sin. I recognize, however, that most churches, even if they offer small-group opportunities, do not structure the groups in this way. So, even if your church doesn't presently offer this, you could still get together with your friends informally.

If you're thinking that getting together with friends is what you'll try to pursue, you could say something like this to them:

> This is not primarily a time for us to chat. It is a time to share openly about our sins or temptations to sin, to point one another to our Savior, to speak of our graces and the way that the Lord is growing us. It's a time for prayer and a time to ask questions about struggles mentioned in the past.

It can happen anywhere: at a coffee house, or in a home, or while taking a walk together. Biblical fellowship doesn't mean that every single time you get together every one of the objectives must be met, but there should be given time for each and the expectation that something more than a superficial visit will be attempted.

YES, BUT . . .

The primary objection to being involved in other people's lives has to do with time. Most people don't think that they have enough time to do what they already need to do. Between their family and work obligations, they already feel stretched to the breaking point. The thought of adding one more obligation is too much. So, first, let me challenge you. If you believe that Christ is calling you to grow, and if you believe that the primary way of growing is through others' ministry in your life, then you'll need to take a very serious look at your schedule to see if you've become activity-oriented instead of people-oriented. Perhaps there are good but unnecessary activities that you could curtail. Even if you can't imagine how time might be made for this kind of fellowship, perhaps you could begin to pray about it.

• Ask yourself, "Am I more interested in attending programs (or watching programs) than I am in relationships with others? Why?"

The second-most-common objection has to do with fear, and primarily the fear of being rejected when trying to help someone with his sin. We're all very aware of the proper boundaries of polite conversation, and biblical fellowship completely ignores them. I'm not encouraging rudeness, but I am encouraging the kind of inquiry that doesn't take a superficial, "Fine, thank you!" for an answer, but asks again, pressing for real transparency. That's why I'm encouraging you to begin by talking to a few close friends and letting them know that you want to pursue this kind of relationship with them. That way, when you start asking probing questions, seeking to draw them out, they won't be put off.

• Ask yourself, "Am I satisfied with superficial answers to questions or do I wisely and humbly seek to draw others out [Prov. 20:5] for the goal of helping them grow in Christ?"

People are also generally afraid that their friends won't like them if they find out how much they struggle with sin. They're afraid of letting the proverbial "cat out of the bag." Of course, the truth is that the cat is already out of the bag and has shredded the curtains. All of our friends are more aware of our sin than we think, and unless we're really living a double life, they could probably tell you what one or two sins you struggle with most and how your sin has personally impacted them. Our struggle with sin is like the party game where everyone else knows the word pinned on your back but you can't see it. The nature of sin is to blind and con us; that's why we need to "exhort one another *every day* . . . that none of [us] may be hardened by the deceitfulness of sin" (Heb. 3:13). Because the gospel has defined everything about who we are, we don't have to pretend we're sinless. We don't have to keep up appearances. There's only one reputation that means anything to us now, and it's not ours. I can afford to look like a sinner because I have a Savior who loves sinners.

• Ask yourself, "Am I transparent about my sin and seeking accountability?"

At a recent conference, I asked the women to get together in small groups and confess sin and ask for help. Afterward one woman told me that she had gotten together with a friend she had known for some years, and instead of confessing some easy outward weakness she asked her friend to tell her what she saw in her life. And her friend loved her enough to do so. She spoke deeply, lovingly, and very pointedly to her about an obvious blind spot. What a great gift! The two of them decided that they're going to hold each other accountable, asking probing questions, praying for each other, seeking to apply Scripture to encourage and comfort.

Faith Working Through Love

Of course, the primary reason we're lethargic about deep biblical fellowship is that we don't love our Savior or our neighbors as we should. We haven't really pondered what he has done for his bride: he laid down his life for her and is pursuing her beautification and adornment. Jesus Christ died for his bride, the church; we've seen what real love looks like, and not only have we seen it, we've experienced it. In fact, "God's love has been poured into our hearts through the Holy Spirit who has been given to us" (Rom. 5:5). When our hearts appear cold and all our motives are self-protective and self-centered, when we're apathetic, we can apprehend by faith what he has said about us. His love has been poured into our hearts through the Holy Spirit. This love is ours and we can begin to pursue one another in faith believing that he will always supply the grace we need.

It is through the church, Paul wrote, that the "manifold wisdom of God might now be made known to rulers and authorities in the heavenly places" (Eph. 3:10). This wisdom was demonstrated through Jesus Christ initially, but it is now being lived out through the church in the lives of every committed believer. As we work out the implications of gospel-centered fellowship, of being sinful and flawed but loved and welcomed, all spiritual powers will know that Christ has, indeed, been victorious. Our lives will be transformed and he will be glorified.

Vacations are wonderful, aren't they? I love being a tourist, visiting a new city, tasting the local fare, seeing new sights. Although we'd all agree that vacations are fun, they aren't real life; that's why they're called "vacations." Real life and real life change are experienced in relationships where we pursue, confess, encourage, confront, and welcome others because we know that our wedding day is approaching and we want the whole family to be ready.

REALIZING HOW GOD'S LOVE TRANSFORMS YOUR IDENTITY AND LIFE

1) The following verses reveal something about gospelized fellowship. Please indicate what it is:
- John 13:33–34
- Romans 12:10, 16

- Ephesians 4:2, 32
- James 5:16

2) Considering your relationships with other Christians, would you say that you are more like a tourist, a student, or a member of a family? What basis is there for your assessment?

3) Is there someone in your life with whom you have gospelized fellowship? If so, who? Are there ways you could be more intentional about your times together? If there isn't someone like that in your life, why isn't there? What are the concerns that would stop you from pursuing this kind of relationship? How would remembering the gospel, "I am more sinful and flawed than I ever dared believe, more loved and welcomed than I ever dared hope," change your perspective on relationships?

4) Summarize in four or five sentences what you've learned from this chapter.

CHAPTER TWELVE

THE HOPE OF THE GOSPEL

". . . not shifting from the hope of the gospel."

COLOSSIANS 1:23

I began this book by posing this question: in your pursuit of godliness have you left Jesus behind? And so, even now, at the end of our study, I'm going to continue to encourage you to remember him and persist in seeking and acknowledging him as long as you have breath. There is only one reason that I long for you to fervently pursue this: the preeminence of Jesus Christ. Because he is preeminent, he is to be supreme in our every thought, word, and deed. He is to be supreme in our hearts because he is supreme in reality. Of course, whether you or I acknowledge him, right now he is the reigning King of all that is, not an afterthought or nice-but-secondary player in the grand scheme of the Father. He is the One at the center of all things. He is the reason we are.

Paul describes his towering superiority in Colossians 1:

He is the image of the invisible God, the firstborn of all creation. For by him all things were created, in heaven and on earth, visible and invisible, whether thrones or dominions or rulers or authorities—all things were created through him and for him. And he is before all things, and in him all things hold together. And he is the head of the body, the church. He is the beginning, the firstborn from the dead, that in everything he might be preeminent. For in him all the fullness of God was pleased to dwell, and through him to reconcile to himself all things, whether on earth or in heaven, making peace by the blood of his cross. (Col. 1:15–20)

In order to help you think more deeply about this familiar passage, here's a paraphrase:

> We look at this Son and see the God who cannot be seen. We look at this Son and see God's original purpose in everything created. For everything, absolutely everything, above and below, visible and invisible, rank after rank after rank of angels—everything got started in him and finds its purpose in him. He was there before any of it came into existence and holds it all together right up to this moment. And when it comes to the church, he organizes and holds it together, like a head does a body.
>
> He was supreme in the beginning and—leading the resurrection parade—he is supreme in the end. From beginning to end he's there, towering far above everything, everyone. So spacious is he, so roomy, that everything of God finds its proper place in him without crowding. Not only that, but all the broken and dislocated pieces of the universe—people and things, animals and atoms—get properly fixed and fit together in vibrant harmonies, all because of his death, his blood that poured down from the cross. (Col. 1:15–20 MESSAGE)

This is our Savior. This is the One we so frequently forget, the One who seems so ancillary, so passé. Our Father doesn't want us to move on, "maturing" past his Son. In point of fact, our Father is intent that we recognize that he has ordered his universe so that it revolves around his beloved One—not around ourselves, our desires, or even our good works done in his name.

So, let me ask you: *Is he the supremely honored center of your being? Is he the incomparable, unparalleled, unrivaled sun around whom your life orbits?* You know that he won't be unless you intentionally and consistently correct your heart. Without conscious effort he'll slip from his rightful throne and in his place will spring up idols of sinful desires or even splendid vices, those good works we think we're doing for him but are actually using as a way to avoid him.[1] And why would we want to avoid him? Simply because we want the preeminence.

Please don't miss the conflict inherent here. Centering your life on his glory will change everything about you, and it is the one thing that your enemy hates more than anything else. Why? Because he wants your focus on him, and if he can't get you to do that, then he'll be pleased if you focus on yourself, on how you're doing, on the importance of your good works or how you may or may not be changing.

DON'T SHIFT AWAY FROM YOUR HOPE

Paul continues this passage on Christ's preeminence with a description of what he has done for you:

> And you, who once were alienated and hostile in mind, doing evil deeds, he has now reconciled in his body of flesh by his death, in order to present you holy and blameless and above reproach before him, if indeed you continue in the faith, stable and steadfast, not *shifting from the hope of the gospel.* (Col. 1:21–23)

Paul cautions us not to shift away from the hope of the gospel. In order to help you understand his caution, let's begin with a discussion of the "hope of the gospel."

The hope we have in the gospel is that the fullness of God condescended to us in Jesus Christ. We don't have to wonder about the Father's disposition toward us; we don't have to speculate for one moment about our future. We can have a strong and sure hope, because we can see the invisible God by looking at the gospel.

Do you need hope? Look at the tiny baby in a cow trough. See the adult's gentle hands blessing the children. Hear his words of invitation and see those hands pierced with spikes. Contemplate the blood-soaked mud. View the empty tomb and the folded grave clothes. See him rise physically to return to his Father, clothed in human flesh. Anticipate his return on the clouds and your eternal union and reign with him. Don't turn away from the hope of the gospel: Christ is utterly and eternally preeminent. You need this hope to face your day; don't look away to yourself or any other person.

You can experience the hope of the gospel because Jesus Christ, the preeminent Son, became man in order to reconcile you to himself. He has made peace between heaven and earth, between God and man, between your Creator and your rebel heart. How? Through the blood of his cross. Never was there any blood like this. Unsullied, beautiful, precious blood poured out as an offering so that he might bring you near.

On the days when you feel as though you'll never get it, you'll never please him, you're such a failure, you must remember the lavish gift: his great heart pumped blood through his veins and then out his wounds so that he could bless you. This perfect blood streamed down his body and tumbled through space, pooling on the earth beneath his feet. It was trampled on by those who stood below jeering. It mingled with the dirt he had created, and from it grew your hope. And then, on the days when you believe you're finally getting it, finally pleasing him, when you think you can look in satisfaction at your goodness, you'll need to look at that blood even more closely. Take yourself to Calvary and stand there until all your good works seem to you as they really are: vile sludge purified only by his cleansing flow.

The hope of the gospel that must command your continual attention is that our strong Man not only died but has risen again. He is a risen Savior, and that changes everything! The old order of unending death upon death has been reversed. Our confident hope is in life after death—and perhaps for some of us, life after life. But our hope is not only for a bright future. We also have hope because by the very act of rising from the dead our Deliverer annihilated our slavery to sin. We're completely free!

Jesus' ascension gives us hope because we now know, beyond all doubt or suspicion, that the Father and his children are reconciled. He is our kinsman; he is still incarnate. Sitting beside the Father of all that is, is a Man, and our Father gazes upon our form at all times and loves us because of him. Our Savior continually presents our needs to his Father and pleads our innocence, displaying his wounds for all to see. If Jesus were ever tempted to forget about us for a moment, all it would take to remind him would be a glance at his own hands. We, too, are seated there with him, in the throne room of heaven where only spirit beings entered before. He has given us the exalted seat at the feast by taking the lowly seat for himself. Don't ever turn aside from the hope of the gospel.

The hope of the gospel is simply this then: that Jesus Christ, the incarnate Son, was born in a lowly manger, lived a perfect life, suffered from the moment of his first breath, was indescribably shamed and cruelly tortured, and then died without the comfort of his Father or the angels on Calvary's cruel tree. After three days in darkness and the tomb he rose again, still in human flesh, and then after forty days he ascended to the Father. Because of this, we have an entirely new identity, not one based on our accomplishments, our self-respect, the accolades of others, our own good works. We are completely and irrevocably justified; we have been entirely forgiven, reconciled, redeemed. We will have eternal life with him, and everything we go through now is in some way tied to these truths.

What does Paul mean when he cautions us against "shifting from the hope of the gospel"? Simply that we must "ponder anew what the Almighty can do, if with his love he befriend [us]!"[2] We must ponder and be consumed with the thought of his sacrificial love, mercy, and grace. May we never think that pondering the Almighty's love is only for beginners. No one ever moves past the need to learn and then relearn this over and over again.

WHY WE SHIFT AWAY

As ridiculous as it may seem, we're all tempted and frequently fall into shifting away from the gospel. Why would we do such a foolish thing?

We turn from Jesus and forget the gospel when we fail to remember that we've been completely reconciled through the body of his flesh and try to reconcile ourselves to him through our good works. Whenever we try to make up for our failures with proclamations of renewed effort or think that we've got to prove our love for him before he'll love us, we're forgetting that the preeminence belongs to him. How often do we hope that his glory and our glory are the same thing? We demand that he change us so that we can feel good about our accomplishments and so that others will appreciate how hard we're trying. We consistently forget that it's not our own righteousness, good theology, or perfection that draws him near to us. He is the honored One, not us.

> Indeed, I count everything as loss because of the surpassing worth of knowing Christ Jesus my Lord. For his sake I have suffered the loss of all things and count them as rubbish, in order that I may gain Christ and be found in him, not having a righteousness of my own that comes from the law, but that which comes through faith in Christ, the righteousness from God that depends on faith. (Phil. 3:8–9)

We functionally forget the gospel when we lose sight of the fact that Jesus has made peace between us and the Father by the blood of the cross. At every turn when we forget this blood and think that we have to appease God in some way, we're forgetting the gospel, and we'll lose hope. God is completely and unalterably at peace with his children. He speaks his "shalom" over our life—a shalom that brings blessings, not curses, and this astonishing benediction:

> The LORD bless you and keep you; the LORD make his face to shine upon you and be gracious to you; the LORD lift up his countenance upon you and give you peace. (Num. 6:24–26)

God is blessing and keeping us. His face is shining upon us. He is being gracious to us. He has looked with love upon us and brought us peace. How can we be assured that all this is true? We can be sure because his curse rested on his Son. Instead of keeping his Son, he forsook him. The Father hid his face from his Beloved and poured out wrath upon him. He thrust his Son from his presence and turned his back on him. We've got shalom because his soul was crushed.

> Therefore, since we have been justified by faith, we have peace
> with God through our Lord Jesus Christ. . . . For while we were
> still weak, at the right time Christ died for the ungodly. . . . But
> God shows his love for us in that while we were still sinners,
> Christ died for us. (Rom. 5:1, 6, 8)

We forget the gospel when we neglect our adoption and think
that we're still just a hired servant. The Father doesn't let us come
to him on those terms. We will either come as sons or we will stay
with the pigs. He won't let us earn anything from him because there
will be no boasting in his sight. It will either be that Jesus and his
glorious gospel has the preeminence or we will go it on our own.

> And because of him you are in Christ Jesus, who became to us
> wisdom from God, righteousness and sanctification and redemp-
> tion, so that, as it is written, "Let the one who boasts, boast in the
> Lord." (1 Cor. 1:30–31)

And we neglect this glorious gospel when we fail to recognize
his preeminence. How frequently we forget that everything is for
him and about him. We forget that he is to be first, in our honor
and in our worship. Whenever the gospel slips from our conscious
thought, our religion becomes all about our performance, and then
we think everything that happens or will ever happen is about us.
When I forget the incarnation, sinless life, death, resurrection, and
ascension, I quickly believe that I'm supposed to be the unrivaled,
supreme, and matchless one. It's at this point that I'm particularly in
need of an intravenous dose of gospel truth. He is preeminent.

> For from him and through him and to him are all things. To him
> be glory forever. Amen. (Rom. 11:36)

And when I forget the future, the way that he will reign as
the consummate king of all and that I'll reign with him, I begin to
scratch around for glory here. I forget that for him it was suffering
here and glory there, and it's to be the same for me, too. When I
neglect the gospel, I'll want nice vacations and nice compliments

and nice things to make my life nicer. I'll long to be able to compare myself favorably with others and to know that I am successful. I'll look down on those who don't meet my standards, and I'll idolize those who excel. I'll forget that he is preeminent.

> For the love of Christ controls us, because we have concluded this: that one has died for all, therefore all have died; and he died for all, that those who live might no longer live for themselves but for him who for their sake died and was raised. (2 Cor. 5:14–15)

Your First Love

Jesus sent a letter to his church from his throne in heaven. This letter contains specific instructions for his followers. To the church at Ephesus he said:

> "I know your works, your toil and your patient endurance, and how you cannot bear with those who are evil, but have tested those who call themselves apostles and are not, and found them to be false. I know you are enduring patiently and bearing up for my name's sake, and you have not grown weary. *But I have this against you, that you have abandoned the love you had at first. Remember therefore from where you have fallen; repent, and do the works you did at first.* If not, I will come to you and remove your lampstand from its place, unless you repent. Yet this you have: you hate the works of the Nicolaitans, which I also hate." (Rev. 2:2–6)

Our Savior was aware of the work, endurance, and theology of these dear saints. They were energetically persevering in their service for him, but they had a problem. They had abandoned the love they had at first. Is it possible that in all their good works, sound theology, and patient endurance they had forgotten Jesus? Like them, when we forget God's love to us in Christ, our love wanes, and we become focused on ourselves, our work, and our reputation. From there, it's not much of a step to begin to be more concerned with the doctrines of others than with the doctrines of the gospel. I'm not saying that doctrine is unimportant. I love theology, but the ardent study of doctrine is no substitute for the ardent love of Jesus Christ. It's not just that those in the church at Ephesus weren't loving him anymore. No, this lack of love was resulting in a lifestyle that called for repentance and first works. *Failing to concentrate on God's love for us in Christ isn't a trivial thing. It will always eventuate in apathetic living. Only the gospel can so invigorate us that we burn with ardor for him in all that we do.*

What was your Christianity like when you were first saved? I can remember my conversion and the first years of my faith. I was on fire. My theology was poor, at best, but my heart was filled with joyful love. My life was still filled with gross sin, but my works, meager as they were, were pleasing to the Lord because my heart burned with love for him. Because I didn't come to him until my early twenties, I can remember the days before my conversion. They were bleak, hopeless, hate-filled. And then, all of a sudden, I was a new person. And I knew I was loved. And because I was loved by him I was transformed.

How long has it been since you experienced first love and worked with joy the way you did then? How long has it been since you cared more for his person then you did for your reputation? When did you last recognize how much he loved you and then loved him in response? When did you last love your neighbor or speak with joy about your Savior?

I'll admit that I used to look at new Christians almost with disdain. "Look at them," I'd scornfully think. "All happy and full of enthusiasm. Just wait till they've walked this road a while. We'll see how happy they are then." Hateful, satanic thoughts, yes? Where did these thoughts spring from? They came from losing my first love. And why did I lose my first love? I lost it because I had functionally forgotten the gospel and focused on myself and living the Christian life.

Not long ago I was speaking with a dear Christian sister who is serious, erudite, and godly. She's no slouch when it comes to her faith, and she's given her whole life in service to God. When I told her

I was going to write about God's love for us in the gospel she replied, "I have to admit that God's love doesn't really move me much. I don't know why and I wish it did." Because she hadn't thought seriously about the gospel in years, she'd lost the zeal of first love.

KNOWING NOTHING BUT JESUS

When Paul visited the Corinthians, he made a decision about how he would present himself. Would he try to come to them and impress them with his great oratory skills or wisdom? Would he try to show them how successful, strong, and eloquent he was? No, of course not. He made a decision before he came to them that he would "know nothing . . . except Jesus Christ and him crucified."

He did this because he didn't want to be preeminent in their hearts. He wanted to appear to be only what he was. This is Paul's testimony:

> And I was with you in weakness and in fear and much trembling, and my speech and my message were not in plausible words of wisdom, but in demonstration of the Spirit and of power, that your faith might not rest in the wisdom of men but in the power of God. (1 Cor. 2:3–5)

Paul was weak; he was in fear and trembling. His speech and his message weren't impressive. Instead, it was God's power that was to impress them, power demonstrated through the weak and despised message of a crucified Christ. Paul didn't want to clean Jesus up and make him presentable so that the celebrities of the day would add Jesus to their repertoire. The shameful death by crucifixion, the weakness of a naked, humiliated Messiah was the perfect vehicle to demonstrate how great God's power was and the preeminence of his Son. Only a supremely powerful deity could turn the world upside down through a bleeding Messiah. Paul wanted these believers to trust in the power of God alone, so he stripped himself of all that would impress their carnal minds and knew only Jesus.

My, how my heart militates against that message! When I

travel to speak at conferences, I want to be sure that I look like I've got my act together. I don't want to appear weak, sinful, in need. Of course, I don't want to overshadow the message of the cross with disorganization, but I must learn to put my whole trust in his message and then leave the results to him. How is it for you? Perhaps you don't speak at conferences but simply try to lead your children to the Lord. Do they see you as the one who has it all together or do they see your reliance on a crucified Savior? What about at work? Do people recognize that you're relying on the goodness of Another, or do they sense that your primary concern is your reputation?

And so again I ask, have you determined to rest your entire life upon the crucified Christ? We'll only do this if we determine to visit Bethlehem, Calvary, and Jerusalem every day. The gods of our culture tell us to be strong, to try to impress people, to cover over our sin, to keep people at arm's length. But that's not the counsel of the Savior. For our sake he became weak, for our souls he washed feet, for our salvation he was stripped, for our relationship he was deserted. Every day, every day—just the gospel, simply the crucified, risen, and ascended Christ.

IS HIS NAME HEARD?

> The name of Jesus is not only light but food. It is oil without which food for the soul is dry and salt without which it is insipid. It is honey in the mouth, melody and joy in the heart. It has healing power. *Every discussion where his name is not heard is pointless.*[3]

As our time together draws to a close I want to leave you with two simple thoughts. The first thought is that we deprive ourselves of great happiness when we shy away from the gospel. Perhaps we don't know exactly how to articulate how every facet of it transforms the soul, but we do know the Name. Let me propose that you begin today to weave that name into everything you do. Whether you're washing the dishes, washing the car, or humbly washing the feet of your spouse, let his name pour forth from you. Don't worry about sounding simple; after all, the apostle Paul determined to know nothing but a crucified Jesus. Calvin quoted Bernard when he said, "Every discussion where his name is not heard is pointless." Oh, how many pointless, tasteless, flat conversations we've had—even with other believers! How many books and songs and sermons we've partaken of that left us craving, weak, and hungry? How many counseling sessions were vacuous because the focus was solely on our duties, and the gospel was never even mentioned?

I'm not proposing that there's something magical about his name, but as we think even momentarily about him, about his incarnation, sinless life, crucifixion, resurrection, and ascension, the gospel becomes a powerful agent to transform us and give us hope. We have to remember that God has "highly exalted him and bestowed on him the name that is above every name, so that at the name of Jesus every knee should bow . . . and every tongue confess that Jesus Christ is Lord" (Phil. 2:9–11).

A Hand Like Ours

Here's one final thought. We struggle to incorporate the gospel into our speech and lives because the world is too much a part of us. We don't have much of a vision of future grace, of the deep and unending happiness that will be ours when we arrive finally on those golden shores. We forget that when we arrive there at last we won't be greeted by some disembodied spirit, but by a Man.

> "A Hand like this hand shall throw open the gate of new Life to thee!" A human hand will grasp us as we make our way into heaven. We shall be greeted by a face—the face of Jesus—that has a form we recognize. The incarnation continues, and so we are included in the life of God. . . . We are not left alone. Jesus has gone before us in a way we may follow through the Holy Spirit whom he has sent, because the way is in his flesh, in his humanity. Jesus himself is that new and living way. The fully human one has gone within the veil in our name and even in our skin. United to

him by the Spirit, to the one who remains united to us, we may follow where he has gone. [4]

That Man is presently preparing for your arrival. As you contemplate the blessed gospel, you'll find yourself more and more eager to talk of him now and see him then. What joy will be ours! Do we long for heaven so that we can be free of sin and sickness? Yes, of course. But that's not the primary motivation for our longings. The primary motivation is that we will *see him whom our soul loves—the One who has so lovingly transformed our identity and life*!

> For your Maker is your husband, the LORD of hosts is his name; and the Holy One of Israel is your Redeemer, the God of the whole earth he is called. (Isa. 54:5)
>
> "And I will betroth you to me forever. I will betroth you to me in righteousness and in justice, in steadfast love and in mercy. I will betroth you to me in faithfulness. And you shall know the LORD." (Hos. 2:19–20)
>
> "Father, I want those you gave me to be with me, right where I am, so they can see my glory, the splendor you gave me, having loved me long before there ever was a world." (John 17:24 MESSAGE)
>
> Let us rejoice and exult and give him the glory, for the marriage of the Lamb has come. (Rev. 19:7)

REALIZING HOW GOD'S LOVE TRANSFORMS YOUR IDENTITY AND LIFE

1) Do you believe that "every conversation where his name isn't mentioned is meaningless?" Why or why not? How will you begin to work his name and the gospel into your thoughts and then out into your speech?

2) What have you learned about yourself in this study?

3) What have you learned about Christ? About the gospel?

4) Paul wrote, "Therefore, my beloved brothers, be steadfast, immovable, always abounding in the work of the Lord, knowing that in the Lord your labor is not in vain" (1 Cor. 15:58). How can

remembering the gospel make you "steadfast, immovable, always abounding in the work of the Lord"?

5) Summarize in four or five sentences what you've learned from this chapter.

6) Summarize the main thesis of this book and what you believe the Lord has taught you through it. Share your thoughts with someone else.

THE BEST NEWS

I didn't begin to understand the gospel until the summer before my twenty-first birthday. Although I had attended church from time to time in my childhood, I'll admit that it never really transformed me in any significant way. I was frequently taken to Sunday school, where I heard stories about Jesus. I knew, without really understanding, the importance of Christmas and Easter. I remember looking at the beautiful stained-glass windows, with their cranberry red and deep cerulean blue, with Jesus knocking on a garden door, and having a vague sense that being religious was good. But I didn't have the foggiest idea about the gospel.

When adolescence came barging in, my strongest memories are those of despair and anger. I was consistently in trouble, and I hated everyone who pointed that out. There were nights when I prayed that I would be good, or more specifically, get out of whatever trouble I was in and do better, only to be disappointed and angered by the failures of the following day.

Upon graduation from high school at seventeen, I was married, had a baby, and was divorced all before the second decade of my life began. It was during the following months and years that I discovered the anesthetizing effects of drugs, alcohol, and illicit relationships. Although I would have been known as a girl who liked to party, I was utterly lost and joyless, and I was beginning to know it.

At one point, I can remember telling a friend that I felt like I was fifty years old, which, at that point in my life, was the oldest I could imagine anyone being. I was exhausted and disgusted, so I decided to set about improving myself. I worked a full-time job, took a full load at a local junior college, and cared for my son. I changed my living arrangements and tried to start over. I didn't know that the Holy Spirit was working in my heart, calling me to the Son. I just knew that something had to change. Don't misunderstand, I was still living a shamefully wicked life; it's just that I felt like I was beginning to wake up to something different.

At this point, Julie entered my life. She was my next-door neighbor and she was a Christian. She was kind to me and we became fast friends. She had a quality of life about her that attracted me, and she was always talking to me about her Savior, Jesus. She let me know that she was praying for me and would frequently encourage me to "get saved." Although I'd had that Sunday school training, what she had to say was something completely different from what I'd ever remembered hearing. She told me I needed to be "born again."

And so, on a warm night sometime in June of 1971, I knelt down in my tiny apartment and told the Lord that I wanted to be his. At that point, I didn't really understand much about the gospel, but I did understand this: I knew I was desperate, and I desperately believed that the Lord would help me. That prayer on that night changed everything about me. I remember it now, thirty-five years later, as if it were yesterday.

In the words of Scripture, I knew I needed to be saved, and I trusted that he could save me. One man who came in contact with some of Jesus' followers asked this same question: "What must I do to be saved?" The answer was simple: "Believe in the Lord Jesus, and you will be saved."

Very simply, what do you need to believe in order to be a Christian? You need to know that you need salvation, help, and deliverance. You must not try to reform yourself or decide that you're going to become a moral person so that God will be impressed. Because he is completely holy, that is, perfectly moral, you have to give up any idea that you can be good enough to meet his standard. This is the good *bad* news. It's bad news because it tells you that you're in an impossible situation that you cannot change. But it's also good news because it will free you from ongoing cycles of self-improvement that end in ultimate failure.

You also need to trust that what you're unable to do—live a perfectly holy life—he's done for you. This is the good *good* news. This is the gospel. Basically the gospel is the story of how God looked down through the corridors of time and set his love on his people. At a specific point in time, he sent his Son into the world to become fully like us. This is the story you hear about at Christmas. This baby grew to be a man, and after thirty years of obscurity he began to show the people who he was. He did this by performing miracles, healing the sick, raising the dead. He also demonstrated his deity by teaching people what God required of them and continually foretold his coming death and resurrection. And he did one more thing: he claimed to be God.

Because of his claim to be God, the leading religious people, along with the political powers of the day, passed an unjust sentence of death upon him. Although he had never done anything wrong, he was beaten, mocked, and shamefully executed on a cross. He died. Even though it looked like he had failed, the truth is that this was God's plan from the very beginning.

His body was taken down from the cross and laid hastily in a rock tomb in a garden. After three days, some of his followers went to properly care for his remains and discovered that he had risen from the dead. They actually spoke with him, touched him, ate with him. This is the story that we celebrate at Easter. After another forty days, he was taken back up into heaven, still in his physical form, and his followers were told that he would return to earth in just the same way.

I told you that there are two things you need to know and believe. The first is that you need more significant help than you or any other merely human person could ever supply. The second is that Jesus, the Christ, is the person who will supply that help and if you come to him, he will not turn his back on you. You don't need to understand much more than that, and if you really believe these truths, your life will be transformed by his love.

Below I've written out some verses from the Bible for you. As you read them, you can talk to God, just as though he were sitting right by you (because his presence is everywhere!) and ask him for help to understand. Remember, his help isn't based on your ability to perfectly understand or anything that you can do. If you trust him, he has promised to help you, and that's all you need to know for now.

> For all have sinned and fall short of the glory of God. (Rom. 3:23)

> For the wages of sin is death, but the free gift of God is eternal life in Christ Jesus our Lord (Rom. 6:23)

> For while we were still weak, at the right time Christ died for the ungodly. For one will scarcely die for a righteous person—though perhaps for a good person one would dare even to die—but God shows his love for us in that while we were still sinners, Christ died for us. (Rom. 5:6–8)

> For our sake he made him to be sin who knew no sin, so that in him we might become the righteousness of God. (2 Cor. 5:21)

> If you confess with your mouth that Jesus is Lord and believe in your heart that God raised him from the dead, you will be saved. For with the heart one believes and is justified, and with the mouth one confesses and is saved. For the Scripture says, "Everyone who believes in him will not be put to shame." . . . The same Lord is Lord of all, bestowing his riches on all who call on him. For "everyone who calls on the name of the Lord will be saved." (Rom. 10:9–13)

> "Whoever comes to me I will never cast out." (John 6:37)

> Therefore, if anyone is in Christ, he is a new creation. The old has passed away; behold, the new has come. (2 Cor. 5:17)

> "Come to me, all who labor and are heavy laden, and I will give you rest. Take my yoke upon you, and learn from me, for I am

gentle and lowly in heart, and you will find rest for your souls."
(Matt. 11:28–29)

There is therefore now no condemnation for those who are in
Christ Jesus. (Rom. 8:1)

If you'd like to, you might pray a prayer something like this:

> Dear God, I'll admit that I don't understand everything about this,
> but I do believe these two things: I need help and you want to help
> me. I confess that I'm like Elyse and pretty much ignored you my
> whole life, except when I was in trouble or just wanted to feel good
> about myself. I know that I haven't loved you or my neighbor so
> it's true that I deserve to be punished and really do need help. But
> I also believe that you've brought me here, right now to read this
> page because you are willing to help me, and that if I ask you for
> help, you won't send me away empty-handed. I'm beginning to
> understand how you punished your Son in my place and how,
> because of his sacrifice for me, I can have a relationship with you.
>   Father, please guide me to a good church and help me under-
> stand your word. I give my life to you and ask you to make me
> yours. In Jesus' name, Amen.

Let me encourage you now to turn to chapter 5, "Look and
Live!" for a fuller understanding of what it means to believe and
have faith.

Here are two more thoughts. In his kindness, Jesus established
his church so that we can encourage and help each other understand
and live out these two truths. If you know that you need help and
you think that Jesus is able to supply that help, or if you're still ques-
tioning but want to know more, please search out a good church in
your neighborhood and begin to make relationships there. A good
church is one that recognizes that we cannot save ourselves by our
own goodness and that relies wholly on Jesus Christ (and no one
else) for this salvation. You can call around and ask these questions,
or you could even go on the Internet and get a listing of churches
in your area. Most churches offer something called a "Statement of
Faith" on their web site that provides information about its beliefs.

Mormons and Jehovah's Witnesses are not Christian churches, and they do not believe in the gospel (though they might tell you that they do), so you don't want to go to a church that is affiliated with Mormons or Jehovah's Witnesses. Finding a good church is sometimes quite an involved process, so don't be discouraged if you don't succeed right away. Keep trying and believe that God will help you.

Secondly, another factor that will help you grow in this new life of faith is to begin to read what God has said about himself and about us in his Word, the Bible. In the New Testament (the last third or so of the Bible), there are four Gospels, or narratives, about the life of Jesus. I recommend that you start with the first one, Matthew, and then work your way through the other three. I recommend that you purchase a good modern translation, like the English Standard Version, but you can get any version (though avoid a paraphrase) that you're comfortable with and begin reading more right away.

The last request that I have of you is that you contact me through my web site, www.elysefitzpatrick.com, if you've decided that you want to follow Jesus and learn about him from this book. Thank you for taking time to read this little explanation of the most important news you'll ever hear. If you are reading the appendix at the outset, you can continue to read this book now and trust that the Lord will help you understand and become what he wants you to be: a person who's been so loved by him that you're transformed in both your identity and life.

BIBLIOGRAPHY

Augustine, *Restless Till We Rest in You: 60 Reflections from the Writings of St. Augustine.* Compiled by Paul Thigpen. Ann Arbor, MI: Servant Publications, 1998.

Beasley-Murray, Paul. *The Message of the Resurrection.* Downers Grove, IL: InterVarsity, 2000.

Berkouwer, G. C. *Studies In Dogmatics: Faith and Sanctification.* Grand Rapids, MI: Eerdmans, 1952.

Calvin, John. *Calvin: Institutes of the Christian Religion,* 2 vols. Edited by John T. McNeill. Philadelphia, PA: Westminster Press, 1960.

———. *The Institutes of the Christian Religion.* Edited by Tony Lane and Hilary Osborne. Grand Rapids, MI: Baker Books, 1987.

Dawson, Gerrit Scott. *Jesus Ascended: The Meaning of Christ's Continuing Incarnation.* Phillipsburg, NJ: P&R, 2004.

Ensor, John. *The Great Work of the Gospel: How We Experience God's Grace.* Wheaton, IL: Crossway Books, 2006.

Gaffin Jr., Richard B. *By Faith, Not By Sight: Paul and the Order of Salvation.* Waynesboro, GA: Paternoster Press, 2006.

Goldsworthy, Graeme. *The Goldsworthy Trilogy: Gospel and Kingdom, Gospel and Wisdom, the Gospel in Revelation.* Waynesboro, GA: Paternoster Press, 2000.

The Heidelberg Catechism with Scripture Texts. Grand Rapids, MI: Faith Alive Christian Resources, 1989.

Keller, Timothy. Unpublished studies: *Galatians, Romans,* and *Gospel Christianity.*

Lane, Timothy S., and Paul David Tripp. *How People Change.* Winston-Salem, NC: Punch Press, 2006.

Lewis, C. S. *Miracles: A Preliminary Study.* San Francisco: HarperSanFrancisco, 2001.

Morris, Leon. *The Apostolic Preaching of the Cross.* Grand Rapids, MI: Eerdmans, 1965.

———. *The Atonement: Its Meaning and Significance*. Downers Grove, IL: IVP Academic, 1983.

Owen, John. *Communion with God*. Abridged by R. J. K. Law. Carlisle, PA: Banner of Truth, 1991.

Pascal, Blaise. *Mind on Fire: An Anthology of the Writings of Blaise Pascal*. Sisters, OR: Multnomah, 1989.

Parsons, Burk, ed. *Assured by God: Living in the Fullness of God's Grace*. Phillipsburg, NJ: P&R, 2006.

Piper, John. *God Is the Gospel: Meditations on God's Love as the Gift of Himself*. Wheaton, IL: Crossway Books, 2005.

Prime, Derek. *The Ascension: The Shout of a King, the Ascension of Our Lord Jesus Christ and His Continuing Work Today*. Surrey, UK: Day One Publications, 1999.

Ridderbos, Herman. *Paul: An Outline of His Theology*. Translated by John Richard DeWitt. Grand Rapids, MI: Eerdmans, 1975.

Romaine, William. *The Life, Walk and Triumph of Faith*. Cambridge; London: James Clarke, 1970.

Ryle, J. C. *Holiness*. Darlington, UK: Evangelical Press, 1997.

Stott, John. *The Cross of Christ*. Downers Grove, IL: InterVarsity, 1986.

Tozer, A. W. *The Knowledge of the Holy*. San Francisco: HarperSanFrancisco, 1961.

———. *The Pursuit of God*. Camp Hill, PA: Christian Publications, 1998.

———. *The Root of the Righteous*. Camp Hill, PA: Christian Publications, 1986.

———. *Whatever Happened to Worship? A Call to True Worship*. Edited by Gerald B. Smith. Camp Hill, PA: Christian Publications, 1985.

Warfield, B. B. *The Person and Work of Christ*. Edited by Samuel G. Craig. Phillipsburg, NJ: Presbyterian and Reformed, 1950.

The Westminster Confession of Faith.

The Westminster Larger and Shorter Catechisms.

Wright, N. T. *The Resurrection of the Son of God*. Minneapolis, MN: Augsburg Fortress, 2003.

NOTES

CHAPTER 1: REMEMBERING HIS LOVE

1. John Owen, *Of Communion with God*, PC Study Bible, pt. 1, chap. 4 (Biblesoft, 2003), emphasis added.
2. Martin Luther, *Selected Sermons*, PC Study Bible (Biblesoft, 2003).

CHAPTER 2: IDENTITY AMNESIA

1. A. W. Tozer, *Whatever Happened to Worship? A Call to True Worship* (Camp Hill, PA: Christian Publications, 1985), 49.
2. Thanks for this perspective go to Paul David Tripp, who generously donated 15 minutes at the end of a message to introduce me and his audience to this concept.
3. Of course, it's also evident in less serious books, songs, or sermons, but then the whole message of both our identity and calling are missing there.
4. Martin Seligman, *Authentic Happiness: Using the New Positive Psychology to Realize Your Potential for Lasting Fulfillment* (New York: Free Press, 2004), 8.
5. Gerrit Scott Dawson, *Jesus Ascended: The Meaning of Christ's Continuing Incarnation* (Phillipsburg, NJ: P&R, 2004), 124.

CHAPTER 3: THE IDENTITY GIFT

1. Citibank identity theft solutions commercial, 2004.
2. In other words, all of our obedience (response to the imperatives of Scripture) must be accomplished in light of the realities of what God has already done for us in Christ (the indicatives of Scripture). See chapter 7 for a fuller treatment of this topic.
3. Gerrit Scott Dawson, *Jesus Ascended: The Meaning of Christ's Continuing Incarnation* (Phillipsburg, NJ: P&R, 2004), 59.
4. I believe that this definition of the gospel originates with pastor Tim Keller.
5. Gerrit Scott Dawson, *Jesus Ascended*, 159.

6. Blaise Pascal, *"Pensees,"* 417, trans. A. J. Krailsheimer (New York: Penguin Classics, 1995), 121.

CHAPTER 4: THE VERDICT

1. Matthew Henry, *Matthew Henry's Commentary on the Whole Bible*, New Modern Ed. (Peabody, MA: Hendrickson, 1991), 2:36–40.
2. Ibid.
3. Acts 4:28.
4. "Justification is the judicial act of God, by which he pardons all the sins of those who believe in Christ, and accounts, accepts, and treats them as righteous in the eye of the law, i.e., as conformed to all its demands. In addition to the pardon of sin, justification declares that all the claims of the law are satisfied in respect of the justified. It is the act of a judge and not of a sovereign. The law is not relaxed or set aside, but is declared to be fulfilled in the strictest sense; and so the person justified is declared to be entitled to all the advantages and rewards arising from perfect obedience to the law (Rom. 5:1–10)." (Easton's Bible Dictionary, PC Study Bible).
5. Gerrit Scott Dawson, *Jesus Ascended: The Meaning of Christ's Continuing Incarnation* (Phillipsburg, NJ: P&R, 2004), 119.

CHAPTER 5: YOUR INHERITANCE

1. John Bunyan, *The Pilgrim's Progress* (New Kensington, PA: Whitaker, 1981), 137–38, 140–41.
2. Ibid.
3. "I am your portion and your inheritance" (Num. 18:20).
4. Isa. 52:7.
5. John Piper, *God Is the Gospel: Meditations on God's Love as the Gift of Himself* (Wheaton, IL: Crossway Books, 2005), 47.
6. Matt. 8:12; 13:42, 50; 22:13; 24:51; 25:30; Luke 13:28.
7. Ps. 145:9; Matt. 5:45; Acts 14:17.
8. Albert Barnes, *Barnes's Notes on the Old and New Testament* (Biblesoft, 1997, 2003).
9. "The AFCARS Report No. 13 for FY2005," U. S. Department of Health and Human Services, Administration for Children and Families, Administration on Children, Youth and Families, Children's Bureau (http://www.acf.hhs.gov/programs/cb).
10. Martin Luther, *Selected Sermons*, PC Study Bible (Biblesoft, 2003).

11. A. W. Tozer, *The Pursuit of God* (Camp Hill, PA: Christian Publications, 1993), 19.

CHAPTER 6: LOOK AND LIVE!

1. Paul's testimony is that this (and every) Old Testament narrative occurred, in part, as an example to us; that they were written for our instruction. "Now these things happened to them as an example, but they were written down for our instruction, on whom the end of the ages has come" (1 Cor. 10:11–12).

2. That the Israelites didn't understand this concept is clear because they eventually made an idol of the bronze serpent and called it Nehushtan (2 Kings 18:4). This was simply another form of man-centered idolatry, another way to manipulate God and control the world. Looking at a crucifix, wearing a cross around your neck won't save you. Something more is required.

3. John Calvin, *Institutes of the Christian Religion,* ed. Tony Lane and Hilary Osborne (Grand Rapids, MI: Baker Books, 1987), 146.

4. 2 Kings 5:10ff.

5. I'm not saying that we should never examine ourselves. We are, in fact, commanded to do so (1 Cor. 11:28; 2 Cor. 13:5). But the self-examination we're called to must be done in faith, keeping our heart's gaze centered on the cross and on belief in God's love and mercy.

6. A. W. Tozer, *The Pursuit of God: The Human Thirst for the Divine* (Camp Hill: PA, 1993), 85.

7. Johannes Louw and Eugene Nida, eds., *Greek-English Lexicon Based on Semantic Domain* (New York: United Bible Societies, 1988). Used by permission.

8. *The Heidelberg Catechism with Scripture Texts* (Grand Rapids, MI: Faith Alive Resources, 1989). Answer 60, p. 87. The Heidelberg Catechism was originally published in January 1563.

9. A. W. Tozer, *The Pursuit of God,* 83.

CHAPTER 7: BE WHO YOU ARE

1. G. C. Berkouwer, *Studies in Dogmatics: Faith and Sanctification* (Grand Rapids: MI, Eerdmans, 1952), 121.

2. Richard B. Gaffin Jr., *By Faith, Not by Sight: Paul and the Order of Salvation* (Waynesboro, GA: Paternoster Press, 2006), 72.

3. "The imperative is grounded on the reality that has been given with the indicative, appeals to it, and is intended to bring it to full develop-

ment." Herman Ridderbos, *Paul, An Outline of His Theology*, trans. John Richard DeWitt (Grand Rapids, MI: Eerdmans, 1975), 255.

4. *The Westminster Larger Catechism*:

Question 75: What is sanctification?

Answer: Sanctification is a work of God's grace, whereby they whom God has, before the foundation of the world, chosen to be holy, are in time, through the powerful operation of his Spirit applying the death and resurrection of Christ unto them, renewed in their whole man after the image of God; having the seeds of repentance unto life, and all other saving graces, put into their hearts, and those graces so stirred up, increased, and strengthened, as that they more and more die unto sin, and rise unto newness of life.

Question 77: Wherein do justification and sanctification differ?

Answer: Although sanctification be inseparably joined with justification, yet they differ, in that God in justification imputes the righteousness of Christ; in sanctification his Spirit infuses grace, and enables to the exercise thereof; in the former, sin is pardoned; in the other, it is subdued: the one does equally free all believers from the revenging wrath of God, and that perfectly in this life, that they never fall into condemnation; the other is neither equal in all, nor in this life perfect in any, but growing up to perfection.

Question 78: Whence arises the imperfection of sanctification in believers?

Answer: The imperfection of sanctification in believers arises from the remnants of sin abiding in every part of them, and the perpetual lustings of the flesh against the spirit; whereby they are often foiled with temptations, and fall into many sins, are hindered in all their spiritual services, and their best works are imperfect and defiled in the sight of God.

5. Ibid.

6. I first heard these categories from Iain Duguid.

7. "'Do not handle, Do not taste, Do not touch' (referring to things that all perish as they are used)—according to human precepts and teachings? These have indeed an appearance of wisdom in promoting self-made religion and asceticism and severity to the body, but they are of no value in stopping the indulgence of the flesh" (Col. 2:21–23).

8. Richard D. Phillips, "Assured in Christ," in *Assured by God: Living in the Fullness of God's Grace*, ed. Burk Parsons (Phillipsburg, NJ: P&R, 2006), 81.

9. G. C. Berkouwer, *Studies in Dogmatics*, 84.

10. Ibid., 122.

11. Here are some commonly used catch-phrases that serve to demonstrate the confusion in many people's minds about the synergistic relationship between God's work and our work:

   • "I simply need to let go and let God," means, as far as I understand it, that we should stop trying to obey and just relax and let God do his work.

   • "I guess that I continue to fail to obey because I'm trying to obey in the flesh." I surmise that what people mean when they say this is that they think they're trying too hard and not relying on God enough and that's why they continue to fail.

   • "She's so heavenly minded she's no earthly good." I suppose that what is meant is that these people spend all their time in a dreamy state of thought and never get around to actually living out their faith.

   Christians need to understand that it is God who is working in them, causing them to desire to do and to work hard at his good pleasure, and that they respond to this grace with hard work.

12. Eph. 2:1–9: "You were dead in the trespasses and sins in which you once walked, following the course of this world, following the prince of the power of the air, the spirit that is now at work in the sons of disobedience—among whom we all once lived in the passions of our flesh, carrying out the desires of the body and the mind, and were by nature children of wrath, like the rest of mankind. But God, being rich in mercy, because of the great love with which he loved us, even when we were dead in our trespasses, made us alive together with Christ—by grace you have been saved—and raised us up with him and seated us with him in the heavenly places in Christ Jesus, so that in the coming ages he might show the immeasurable riches of his grace in kindness toward us in Christ Jesus. For by grace you have been saved through faith. And this is not your own doing; it is the gift of God, not a result of works, so that no one may boast."

13. Gerrit Scott Dawson, *Jesus Ascended: The Meaning of Christ's Continuing Incarnation* (Phillipsburg, NJ: P&R, 2004), 109 (italics added).

14. *The Belgic Confession*, Article 24: The Sanctification of Sinners, "So then, it is impossible for this holy faith to be unfruitful in a human being, seeing that we do not speak of an empty faith but of what Scripture calls 'faith working through love,' which leads a man to do by himself the works that God has commanded in his Word.

15. "Answer 114," in *The Heidelberg Catechism with Scripture Texts* (Grand Rapids, MI: Faith Alive Christian Resources, 1989), 159.

16. "Answer 86," in *The Heidelberg Catechism with Scripture Texts*, 117 (italics added). The question they were answering was why, if we're completely delivered from our misery by God's grace alone through Christ, must we still do good. I've used their response to answer a different but related question: If I'm never able to do good without failure of some sort, should I try to do it?

17. "Assurance is the conscious confidence that we are in a right relationship with God through Christ. . . . The enjoyment of assurance is simply the inner nature of faith bursting out into our conscious awareness of what it means." Sinclair Ferguson, "Assurance Justified," in *Assured by God*, 98, 102.

18. "The gospel is the only means we have of beginning, continuing and persevering in the Christian life. . . . When we approach sanctification as attainable by any means other than the gospel of Christ—the same gospel by which we are converted—we have departed from the teaching of the New Testament." Graeme Goldsworthy, *The Goldsworthy Trilogy: The Gospel in Revelation* (Waynesboro, GA: Paternoster Press, 2000), 171.

19. John Calvin, *Institutes of the Christian Religion,* ed. Tony Lane and Hilary Osborne (Grand Rapids, MI: Baker Books, 1987), 128.

CHAPTER 8: I WILL CLEANSE YOU

1. There are a number of imperatives in the New Testament that tell us to do nothing more than "consider" something. For instance, we're to consider our own sinfulness: Matt. 7:3; James 1:23–24; God's providence displayed in nature: Luke 12:24, 27; Jesus: Heb. 3:1; 12:3; how to help one another: Heb. 10:24.

2. Herman Ridderbos, *Paul: An Outline of His Theology*, trans. John Richard De Witt (Grand Rapids, MI: Eerdmans, 1975), 209.

3. Ibid.

4. Ibid.

5. John Calvin, *Romans and Thessalonians*, trans. Ross Mackenzie (Grand Rapids, MI: Eerdmans, 1991), 167 (italics added).

6. C. S. Lewis, *Miracles* (San Francisco: Harper San Francisco, 1947), 175.

7. *hēdone*, from *handano* (to please); sensual delight; by implication, desire; KJV lust, pleasure, *Biblesoft's New Exhaustive Strong's Numbers and Concordance with Expanded Greek-Hebrew Dictionary* (Biblesoft and International Bible Translators, 1994, 2003).

8. *epithumeō*, to set the heart upon, i.e., long for (rightfully or otherwise); KJV covet, desire, would fain, lust (after), *Biblesoft's New Exhaustive Strong's Numbers and Concordance with Expanded Greek-Hebrew Dictionary*.

9. Blaise Pascal, *Pensees,* 148, trans. A. J. Krailsheimer (New York: Penguin Classics, 1995), 45.

10. C. S. Lewis, *The Weight of Glory and Other Addresses* (San Francisco: HarperSanFrancisco, 2001), 26.

11. "You have made us for yourself, and our hearts are restless till they find their rest in you. . . . What tortuous ways I walked! Woe to that rash soul of mine, that hoped by abandoning you, Lord, to find something better! It tossed and turned, upon its back, upon its sides, upon its belly, yet it found every place it lay to be hard—you alone are my rest. And behold, you are near at hand, and you deliver us from our wretched wanderings, and you settle us in your own way. And you comfort us, saying: 'Run, I will carry you; yes, I will lead you to the end of your journey, and there also I will carry you.'" Augustine, *Restless Till We Rest in You: 60 Reflections from the Writing of St. Augustine,* comp. Paul Thigpen (Ann Arbor, MI: Servant Publications, 1998), 18–19.

12. William Romaine, *The Life, Walk and Triumph of Faith* (London: James Clarke, 1970), 280.

CHAPTER 9: WALK IN LOVE

1. Margaret Wise Brown and Clement Hurd, *Runaway Bunny* (New York: Harper and Row, 1972).

2. This doesn't mean that our desire for love is neutral, like a love cup that needs to be filled. No, it means that we make idols out of those things God gives us as a good; we want them so much we're willing to sin in order to possess them.

3. William Romaine, *The Life, Walk and Triumph of Faith* (London: James Clarke, 1970), 165.

4. By the way, if there's anything in the world that I don't need to be taught, it's how to love myself. I know just what I want and I know

how to serve myself so that I can get it. Even if I spend every day in self-loathing, it isn't a sign of a lack of self-love. No, just the opposite is true. None of the writers of the New Testament, and especially not our Savior himself, ever thought for one moment that our problem was that we didn't love ourselves enough. No, our problem is *always* that we love ourselves too much and we're far too focused on making sure we get what we want or punishing ourselves and others when we don't.

5. Gerrit Scott Dawson, *Jesus Ascended: The Meaning of Christ's Continuing Incarnation* (Phillipsburg, NJ: P&R, 2004), 94.

6. Ibid., 182. Quoted from John Calvin, *The Deity of Christ and Other Sermons,* trans. Leroy Nixon (Audubon, NJ: Old Paths Publications, 1997), 238–39.

CHAPTER 10: TAKE COURAGE; YOUR SINS ARE FORGIVEN

1. John Stott, "The Cross of Christ," in Rowan Williams, *Eucharastic Sacrifice* (Downers Grove, IL: InterVarsity, 1986), 272 (italics added).

2. See Matthew 14:27; Mark 6:50. He also uses it in John 16:33: "I have said these things to you, that in me you may have peace. In the world you will have tribulation. But take heart; I have overcome the world."

3. While drawing out some of these situations, I'm not thinking of any one person in particular, although I am drawing on my experience as a counselor.

CHAPTER 11: GOSPEL-CENTERED RELATIONSHIPS

1. John Piper, "How Christ Enables the Church to Build Itself Up in Love" (September 17, 1995), sermon found at Desiring God resource library (http://www.desiringGod.org.).

2. For a deeper explanation of this topic, please see my *Helper by Design: God's Perfect Plan for Women in Marriage* (Chicago: Moody Press, 2003). Of course there are times when it is good to be alone for short seasons to seek the Lord. There are also times when aloneness cannot be avoided: when away from home, when ill. These times are particularly trying because we weren't meant to be alone. Life on a desert island is dreadful even if one has an abundance of food and water.

CHAPTER 12: THE HOPE OF THE GOSPEL

1. David Brainard:

> When I had been fasting, praying, obeying, I thought I was aiming at the glory of God, but I was doing it all for my own glory—to feel I was worthy. As long as I was doing all this to earn my salvation, I was doing nothing for God, all for me! I realized that all my struggling to become worthy was an exercise in self-worship. I was actually trying to avoid God as saviour, and to be my own saviour. . . . I was not worshipping him, but using him. . . . Though I often confessed to God that I, of course, deserved nothing, yet still I harbored a secret hope of recommending myself to God by all theses duties and all this morality. In other words, I healed myself with my duties.

George Whitefield:

> Our best duties are as so many splendid sins. Before you can speak peace to your heart you must not only be sick of your original and actual sin, but you must be made sick of your righteousness, of all your duties and performances. There must be a deep conviction before you can be brought out of your self-righteousness; it is the last idol taken out of our heart. The pride of our heart will not let us submit to the righteousness of Jesus Christ.

> *On the Method of Grace* (http://www.bartleby.com/268/3/20.html). Both the Brainard and Whitefield quotes were presented in a sermon by Pastor Mark Lauterbach.

2. "Praise to the Lord, The Almighty," Lyrics: Joachim Neander, in *A und Ω Glaub-und Liebesübung* (Stralsund: 1680); translated from German to English by Catherine Winkworth, 1863.

3. John Calvin, *The Institutes of the Christian Religion*, ed. Tony Lane and Hilary Osborne (Grand Rapids, MI: Baker Books, 1987), 128 (italics added).

4. Gerrit Scott Dawson, *Jesus Ascended: The Meaning of Christ's Continuing Incarnation* (Phillipsburg, NJ: P&R, 2004), 7.

Order at: www.b4tmusic.com/becausehelovesme

or call: 240 • 393 • 3635

Email: beforethethronemusic@aol.com

Retail: $5.99

Shipping: $2.99 (no quantity limit)